WITH A B.-P. SC
A RECORD OF THE

CW00521386

EDMUND YERBURY PRIESTMAN,
BORN FEBRUARY 25TH, 1890.
FELL IN ACTION NOVEMBER 19TH, 1915.

Frontispiece.]

WITH A B.-P. SCOUT

IN

GALLIPOLI

A RECORD OF THE BELTON BULLDOGS

BY

E. Y. PRIESTMAN

Scoutmaster of the 16th (Westbourne) Sheffield Boy Scouts

WITH REPRODUCTIONS FROM THE AUTHOR'S ORIGINAL SKETCHES

AND A FOREWORD BY

LIEUT.-GENERAL SIR ROBERT BADEN-POWELL
C.B., C.V.O.

TO

JIMMY

SOMEWHERE IN ENGLAND

THIS BOOK

AND

ALL IT MAY EARN

ARE

DEDICATED

FOREWORD

THE cheery notes which form this book will appeal
to every reader as directly illustrating how
practice of the Boy Scout ideals will help a man to
face the Great Adventure.

The author was himself one of the Brotherhood
of Scouts, and as such he had learnt that, in
addition to Common-sense and Cunning, Cheerful-
ness and Courage constitute the important C's
towards successful soldiering; and these, his
letters show, he practised to the full.

The sudden end of this very lovable and much
alive personality is impressive in its warning to
the reader himself to practise the Scouts' Motto,
" For life or death to Be Prepared."

ROBERT BADEN-POWELL.

INTRODUCTION

Edmund Yerbury Priestman, the author of the following letters and sketches, was one of those rare people who combine a great tenderness and gentleness with a keen sense of humour and a saving common sense. He had fine artistic and poetic gifts. His common sense saved him from drifting into dreamy and inconclusive habits of life which would have been the danger with many men of his temperament. After leaving school he entered business. All his spare time was given to work in the Boy Scout Movement and Men's Adult Schools. These efforts led him to a life of devotion seldom surpassed. It is not the purpose of this Introduction to give details of his work, but it must be recorded that hundreds of boys and men will remember as long as they live that they owe to his leadership the habit and inspiration of a good life.

At the outbreak of war he placed himself at the disposal of the Sheffield Watch Committee to superintend the Boy Scouts who were guarding places of danger from spies, his daily round covering eighty miles. As soon as this work could be left he took a commission (October, 1914) in the 6th Battalion of the York and Lancaster Regiment. After nine months' training at Belton Park, Grantham, and Witley Camp, Godalming, he went out and was in the Suvla Bay landing of August 6th, 1915, and fell on the night of November 18th-19th, 1915, in defending an advanced post for the holding of which he had volunteered.

He was twenty-five years of age.

Capt. Toohey of the same Battalion wrote the following letter :

York and Lancaster Regiment,
Rugeley Camp,
Staffordshire.
February 11*th*, 1916.

ED. PRIESTMAN, ESQR.

SIR,

I was glad to receive your letter. Few of us were spared. The bravest and best were taken. Many died without having had a chance to show their valour, but your son has given us an example which will live in the history of the Regiment. He was an honest, keen, clean-minded English gentleman and died worthily.

The sergeant's letter states : " The sad affair

cast a gloom over the whole camp. His thoughts were always with his men and they had the greatest respect for him." I would add to this that his fellow officers also had the greatest respect for him, and his seniors the highest confidence in his ability.

It were impertinence to offer condolence.

I congratulate you on being the father of this gallant officer.

Believe me, sir,

Yours most sincerely,

W. H. TOOHEY
(Captain, 6th Batt. York and Lancaster Regt.)

J. H. DONCASTER.

SHEFFIELD,
   June 2nd, 1916.

CONTENTS

xi

LIST OF ILLUSTRATIONS

xiv   LIST OF ILLUSTRATIONS

Foyles Bookshop
113-119 Charing Cross Rd
London WC2H 0EB
Tel: 020 7437 5660
Academic Bookseller of the year.
Now also at the Royal Festival Hall

TEL NO: 020 7437 5660
VAT NO: 239 28 2 3

No refund/exchange

PREFACE

January 10*th*, 1915.

MY DEAREST MOTHER,

You told me that for some strange reason (known only to yourself) you keep all my letters, so the conviction has been " brought home to me of late " as the Quakers say, that if anyone *should* ever come to look through the mighty pile which must have accumulated by now, they will be distressed to find how uncommonly wanting in style and interest they all are. I have decided to reform, however, and should suggest that you start a new file entitled :

HUNS IN THE MAKING

OR

THE BELTON BULLDOGS

(LETTERS OF A SUBALTERN IN KITCHENER'S ARMY, 1915.)

Well, here goes :

CHAPTER I

LIFE IN BELTON

CHAPTER I

Angel and Royal Hotel,
Grantham.
January 10th, 1915.

AFTER my last glimpse of civil (and civilised) life, I found Belton, as I have already told you, in a state of indescribable misery and mud. The sole geological expert among us has ventured the suggestion that the soil is of a clayey nature which is liable to hold the water to a certain degree. This is a valuable suggestion, of course, but when it comes to the question of how to get rid of the pools of stagnant liquid which are formed every time anyone draws his foot out of the said clay, our expert has no idea to offer. The only man on the premises who has turned his genius on to the subject with any practical effect is the mess cook, who was seen scooping up bucketsful which afterwards appeared on the officers' table in the guise of alleged oxtail soup.

B 2

8

When, during a single night, the Quartermaster's stores, the Colonel's horse, half a ton of coal and a Lance-Corporal all sank out of sight, matters became almost serious, and on Monday we set out for a route march, quite hoping that when we got back there might be no huts available at all.

It was lucky, by the way, that our first day's work was a route march, as most of us had come back here feeling in no fit condition to do any serious brain-work ; and a fifteen-mile march doesn't over-tax the mind, whatever may be the effect on the legs.

Unfortunately the first village of any size we came to we were halted and the subalterns were told that they were to act as though we were out at the Front and were going to billet our men for the night. This, of course, meant interviewing the inhabitants and finding what rooms they had available.   I cast my eye upon a row of cottages—

Knocking at the door of No. 1, I found I had drawn the village idiot—or rather his grandam, from whom he evidently inherited his intellect. It took me a quarter of an hour, with the assistance of the company Sergeant-Major and a pint-mug, to bring the old lady out of hysterics, and another twenty minutes to explain that we were only practising and didn't want to hide from the Germans under her bed. She *had* one small bedroom,

John Hogg   Jane Hogg   Bella Hogg (aged 2)   Jimmy Hogg (aged 6)

Andrew Hogg (Uncertain age.)   One of the Hogg lodgers

however, so I billeted a corporal and three men on her hospitality. As one man expressed it: " There's fleas as big as black-clocks jumpin' off 'er, sir ! " But what odds ? We must be getting used to these little things. Such adversity will make men of us. (I am billeted in the local hotel.)

The next cottage was the home of the Hogg family.

But they had too many lodgers already, and I decided the best thing to do under the circumstances was to prevent overcrowding, so we gave them a " miss."

Passing on somewhat hurriedly I overheard our Captain holding converse with an elderly spinster. His part of the argument was " But, my dear madam !—" and hers was to the effect that although she herself was out on Tuesdays and Fridays, as she always went over to Little Gunnerby, four miles away, twice a week to see her brother's wife's mother, who was a cripple with rheumatics, if we did want to use her house (she simply could *not* grasp the fact that we were only practising) we could find the key at the second house on the left down the next side street but four, though the front door lock was unfortunately broken by the butcher-boy when he came for his Christmas-box—you know what these country boys are ! The back door, however, was all right if you gave it a good shove . . . . At this point the Captain fled.

Well, such is the life we are living.

One more incident and then I must stop. I was talking to a man about the knives I gave out to my men at Christmas, and he said he'd no use for can-openers ; he always used dinner-knives to open tins of meat.

" But don't you ever break the blades ? " I asked him.

" Yes—always ! " said he.

CHAPTER II

MULES

CHAPTER II

MULES

Angel and Royal Hotel
Grantham.
January 17th, 1915.

TWENTY of them arrived on Tuesday, and after a twelve hours' journey without changing, and ten of them to each cattle-truck, they felt rather tired and more than rather cross.

Their real purpose in life is to act as light draft animals, but they seem to have developed ideas of their own about their duties which seem to be confined to kicking holes in the huts and biting their unhappy grooms. They look like nothing on earth, and it was quite a toss-up whether we had anyone in camp capable of training them to do anything. But a thought occurred to the Colonel which has solved matters to some extent. He suggested that as we had twenty subalterns with nothing to do, and twenty mules that wanted training, we should introduce one to the other. So

11

any afternoon you may see us trotting about the parade ground on these nightmare nags. Only one casualty has happened yet, and that was so funny to watch that the victim himself (when he came round) saw the humour of it. Well, he might have known that when he got on the beast there would be trouble. I mean, it *looked* all wrong to begin with—

I must say the roll in the brute's eye would have warned me, but his natural history was weak and he took the job on. I saw him come off and it was rather wonderful. The mule shook its ears, looked round, bit him, bent all its knees and went ahead like steam at a level about two feet below where he was sitting, leaving him in mid-air. He didn't stay there long, however, and it was lucky there was a patch of deep mud where he came to earth again.

One afternoon we had just got in from a route march, with the band in front as usual, and the mules were coming out of their stables on to the parade ground just as we dismissed. Our big drummer, who is a humorist (being also an Irishman) crept up behind a huge mule ridden by a small and nervous groom and whacked his drum suddenly and loudly. Of course the animile flew seventeen ways at once and the groom hung on like grim death. As he cantered past my platoon —the " BOOM ! " of the drum still echoing in the air—our humorist remarked : " What a 'orrid 'ard kick yer *must* 'ave given the pore beast ! "

Talking of route marches, we were on a short one yesterday and the same platoon humorist was luckily in the first rank, just behind me. At one place we passed an aged and decayed yokel—of some ninety summers—whom our funny man greeted with : " Hello, young 'un ! Playing truant again ? "

Further on we passed the lines of the South Staffords, who were off duty and lined the wall to jeer at us accordingly. A row of them were particularly cutting, but retired when our comedian remarked : " My word, look at the lady-killers ! "

"My word, look at the lady-killers!"

Well, they certainly weren't handsome, but there was no need to be rude.

There has been a good strong wind for the last few days and the mud is drying nicely, so you needn't bother about me. I never felt more fit.

CHAPTER III

SARTOR RESARTUS, ETC.

CHAPTER III

SARTOR RESARTUS, ETC.

Angel and Royal Hotel,
Grantham.
January 31*st*, 1915.

HAVING told us for the past month that we might be warned to pack up and go at any instant, it has just occurred to the authorities that it might be as well to teach the junior officers a few principles of elementary strategy, so they have turned four of us loose under the care of a staff officer fresh from the Front for the last week. As the work has been mostly theoretical, there isn't much to tell. In fact, the first three days were so much like school that the sooner they are forgotten the better. I mean, we were all cribbing off one another and bobbing our hands up and saying : " Please, sir, I know, sir ! " Horrid !

On Thursday, however, we had to do a bit of reconnaissance over a given stretch of ground. This, presumably, was arranged to keep us good while our instructor took a rest. Anyway he didn't turn up. So we went over the ground and made notes and got through as quickly as possible and then two of us set out for a joy-ride on my motor-bike and side-car.

Here the horrors commence. Whirling round a corner in a small village, we came upon a cluster of officers all making sketches and taking notes just like a lot of Sunday-school kids on a natural history outing. Of course we pulled up to see what they were up to. We thought it was some of our party and prepared to jeer. However, as the old bike slid along in a cloud of dust and pulled up with a grunt, we found to our horror we were slap under the noses of our own Colonel and Major ! Which couple looked the more foolish I don't know : we who had to try to look unconcerned with the half-spoken jeers hot upon our lips, or they who had been caught (after all the pains they had taken to make us think they knew *everything*, too), taking notes in absurd little notebooks while OUR *own* Staff Officer told them what to write.

I doubt if Napoleon was ever caught in a delicate situation like that, but certainly he never acted more promptly.

Pretending not to have seen the Colonel and

Major, we got off the bike and calmly walked up to the Staff Officer and handed in our reports of the morning's work. The General was with him, and, after a cheery little chat with them, we rode away without so much as glancing at our old Colonel. It was just like dropping into a class of small boys and going to speak to the master. Naturally you ignore the pupils.

Awful sick man, our Colonel. Likewise the Major. But rather a gloat for us !

We got another new lot of recruits in last week. One is fat and foolish and he has already made his name.

The first thing he did was to *clean his boots !* This may seem quite a natural thing to anyone who hasn't seen Belton Park, but it brought a crowd of scoffers round the unhappy man in no time. As one of them said : " If tha's got them 'igh society notions in thi —— 'ead they didn't ought to 'a' let thi out o' Buckingham Palace."

They also tell him the most outrageous yarns, all of which he believes. For instance, one of the men, who was a coal-miner before joining the Army, was saying that in their pit they always used donkeys to carry the coal, because it was more accurate.

" 'Ow do yer mean—' ackirate ' ? " said the new recruit.

" Why," said the ex-miner, " you see, when they'd loaded up a basket on to the donkey's back they used to watch it careful, and as soon as ever they'd got *exactly* a ton of coal on it—no more and no less—the donkey would wave its tail once. As soon as they'd put in another ton it would waggle its tail twice, until they'd got up to nine tons. Every donkey carried ten tons, you see."

" Well, why didn't it wag its tail ten times for the tenth ton ? " asked the simple recruit.

" Well, you see, the other nine baskets pretty nearly covered it all over," said the old soldier, " and they 'ad to tie the last one on its tail.   Now yer can't expect it ter wag a ton about, *can* yer ? "

CHAPTER IV

"LITTLE DROPS OF WATER, LITTLE GRAINS OF
SAND"

CHAPTER IV

" LITTLE DROPS OF WATER, LITTLE GRAINS OF SAND "

Angel and Royal Hotel,
Grantham.
February 7th, 1915.

(THE little grains of sand really come first, and the little drops of water more towards the end of the week, but never mind.)

As I said last week, it has just struck some genius in our midst that we may be going to fight the Germans soon and it might therefore be helpful to us to know how to dodge the bullets which they will possibly fire at us when they have got over their first paroxysms of astonishment at seeing us form fours.

So it was decreed that we should sally forth one evening and " dig ourselves in " with picks and shovels. Most trenches at the Front, by the way, are dug in the dark.

So we did indeed sally forth, and by the time the

25

shades of night had just reached their murkiest, arrived at the scene of operations. Exactly *how* a trench is dug dead straight and the same width from end to end is a secret which the British Army guards jealously and I may not reveal, but the process includes a good deal of moistening the hands and evil language. Of course no lights of any kind are allowed and swearing has to be done in a whisper, so it's really one thing on top of another—sickening.

We got back to camp at 12.30 a.m., and were up again soon after that. But we keep cheerful through it all.

The next day we spent actually in our trench, two feet broad and six feet deep.

We had nothing to do, and every time we showed a head another battalion fired blank cartridges at us. But we got through the day somehow, and marched back to the strains of all the latest pantomime songs and that stirring hymn (to the tune of the Sankey hymn, " Looking this Way ") :

> " Kitchener's Army : working away
> Like bloomin' niggers : for one bob a day,
> Every morning : the Officers say,
> ' Put 'im in t' guard room : forfeit 'is pay.' "

Our company has been taken over by the Major, as our late commander has been transferred to

the machine-gun section,   The new man is making
the fur fly and we shall all be smarter for it soon,
though I fear at least half D Company will over-
stay their week-end passes this week.

I overheard our Quartermaster-Sergeant talking
to my Platoon Sergeant yesterday. He said :
" The Major wants a list of Babtisses and Wes-
leyans and all such things in the company."
Rather well expressed, I thought.

Yesterday I saw one of the funniest things I've
seen yet, and he was in at it.   He isn't handsome,
to say the least of it, being rather like this—

Also he is quite small.   Well, yesterday he was
standing at the door of the dining-hall while the
men filed in for dinner.   He had spoken severely to
several of them for crowding each other in their
eagerness to get in, and evidently the men at the
end of the line had fixed up a scheme for him, for (to
my utter astonishment, needless to say), a great

bulky corporal, when his turn came, gently put his hands on the Sergeant's shoulders and *kissed* him on the cheek, while the men following each chucked him under the chin ! (Collapse of the Sergeant, who couldn't very well enter up a charge-sheet to say he had been kissed !) Please don't think this is a sample of the discipline of Kitchener's First Army. Kissing sergeants is rather the exception than the rule.

A solemn and dingy person met me in the officers' mess lounge the other day and asked if he might have the honour of taking my photograph for nothing. I asked him what for. He said : " I'm from the Press Association." " Yes," I said, " but what do you want my photo for ? " To which he replied in a sepulchral whisper : " Obishewry List ! " I told him to go and ask the Major, and later on I saw two men burying something at the bottom of the camp. So I suppose he found the Major.

As a matter of fact, the best authorities all think that I shall live to do great things. For instance, I have several small friends in the village where I keep the motor-bike (in fact it is rather embarrassing when the battalion is marching through to have John Edward, and William Henery, and Wally, and George and Ernest and Nevil, *all* line up and greet " Mist' Pleeeman ! " as we go by) ; and one of them, John Edward, I think, said to Wally : " Mist' Pleeeman's a kurnill, ain't you, Mist' Pleeeman ? "   I told him I wasn't a colonel yet, to which he replied :   " Oo !   But I bet yer soon *will* be ! "

CHAPTER V

ONE THING AND ANOTHER

CHAPTER V

THE BELTON BULLDOGS

ONE THING AND ANOTHER

Grantham.
February 21*st*, 1915.

EXCEPT for one burst of frantic energy we've done very little this week (considering we *are* Kitchener's Army). We've got a shooting course coming on next week and we have been practising rapid-loading in our huts mostly. But the one gorgeous burst is worthy of a special dispatch to itself.

It was a large field-day in which a whole brigade took part. We were told that the enemy would be occupying a ridge and some woods and we were to drive them out. D Company was told off for the firing line, and my platoon occupied a prominent place in the centre.

After a four-mile route march, which was conducted in the quiet, courageous manner typical of the British soldier going into action (at least six new and entirely imprintable verses were added to the already long Company Marching Song), we reached our point of " deployment."

To " deploy " means simply to branch off to the flank at a given point, regardless of hedges or other little hindrances. (The pair of breeches I ordered to replace those left fluttering by the roadside haven't come yet. It's cold, too!) At this point the Major left his horse and directed the attack on foot. He was sorry later on. Once away from the road we were ordered to adopt " artillery formation," which is like this—

```
                ....            ....
                ....            ....
    No. 14      ....   No. 13   ....   (US)
                ....            ....
                ....            ....
                ....            ....


                ....            ....
    No. 16      ....   No. 15   ....
    Platoon     ....            ....
                ....            ....
                ....            ....
                ....            ....
                ....            ....
```

Across the first field we kept this formation beautifully.

Then we met a second hedge and then a wet

"SOME OF MY PLATOON RESTING BY THE ROADSIDE ON A ROUTE MARCH."

ploughed field.   On switching my attention from
the ground to the platoon in front I found (by some
unexplained means) they had disappeared and left
not a sign of themselves !   At this point a head
poked up over a hedge and saw me—and wanted
to know what the ---- I thought I was doing ?
To which I replied that I was under the impression
that I was advancing in artillery formation.   On
closer examination I found my formation was more
like a Mothers' Meeting out for a walk, owing to
the " tactical features " of the ground (*i.e.*, the
furrows)—

Well, the Colonel (for the head belonged to no
less !) cursed me and my Mothers' Meeting most
vilely for ten minutes and then went in search of
the Major to repeat the best bits over again to him.
The engagement was now developing rapidly and
the enemy's artillery (represented by blue flags on
the hill) was dropping shrapnel into us with deadly
effect.   However, we pushed on nobly, in the hopes
of finding the Colonel and Major in death-grips
further on.   More ploughed fields and a brook

some eight feet broad—which we were just in time
to see the Major jump into—brought us into open
ground within range of the enemy's infantry fire
(red flag). Some half-mile of sloping " plough "
had now to be negotiated, so I marshalled my
gallant band and prepared to rush the heights in
extended order.

To my surprise I found that I was now commanding a mixture of my own men, the West
Yorks, the Machine Gun Section, and the Army
Service Corps ! However, they were all food for
powder, so we carried on. (It appeared later that
the Colonel himself had taken over most of my
platoon and got it taken prisoner !)

Ten minutes later the enemy was in full retreat
and we were after them. On my right, hidden by
a wall, was the Colonel of the West Yorks, and my
command had now resolved itself into about twenty
of his men on *my* side of the wall. At this point a
voice, almost hysterical in its enthusiasm, instructed
me to take my choice between everlasting torment
or doing what it told me.

" *Will* you go to —— or *will* you do as I tell
you ? "

As it hadn't told me to do *anything* I
asked it what it wanted. It (the Adjutant this

time) replied : " Send out scouts to keep touch with the enemy ! " I pointed out that these weren't my men, and that their colonel was over the wall. An unrepeatable interlude followed. I sent out scouts.

Enter the West Yorks Colonel and wants to know who in the name of Beelzebub put me in charge of *his* men ? I had presence of mind to whistle up the stretcher-bearers, and retired. The life of a subaltern is hard.

Three miles of ploughed fields at the " double," two rivers and a railway cutting with perpendicular sides, and then, at the moment of victory, to get wiped out like that ! But 'twas a famous victory !

The last lot of recruits is progressing slowly and still are a bright spot in our dreary lives. The sergeant in charge of them had been rather more forcible than usual with one squad the other day, and the following dialogue took place (I'm told) :

Sergt. You're a lot of useless blanky blanketty blankers, and the only man who's any good at all is Smithers. 'E *can* drill a bit. It's a pleasure to drill Smithers. Is there anything you'd like me to do for you, Smithers ? It's a pleasure to encourage the only man of you who's better than a sanguinary rat at his drill !

Smithers puts in a claim for the Victoria Cross.

Sergt.   Now, Smithers, you know the V.C. is only given in *very* special cases of bravery.   I can't do it for you, you know !

Smithers.   Well, then, 'ave you a old pair of *trowsers* you've done with ?

CHAPTER VI

FLITTING

CHAPTER VI

THE BELTON BULLDOGS—*Continued*

FLITTING

Witley Camp,
Godalming,
Surrey.
April 11*th*, 1915.

ON Monday morning—or rather in the middle of Sunday night (about 6 a.m., to be exact), we shook off the dust of Belton from our feet for ever and turned our faces southward to the strains of " Tipperary," rendered with much feeling by the band. It was a stirring moment, and a great sigh of thankfulness was only checked by the Sergeant-Major just in time to stop its reaching the likeness of a cheer.

For the first three miles we just felt cheerful and grateful for the change which had come at last, after so many months of waiting ; but at Grantham we had our first taste of hero-worship and we've not been the same since. The streets were lined with

41

spectators, who were evidently under the impression that our first halt would be at Ypres or somewhere. At any rate the female portion of the crowd wept madly into Union Jack handkerchiefs and the male portion stifled manly sobs as they wished us all sorts of encouraging things between the sniffs. Altogether a very moving spectacle, and a most valuable one, as it bucked the men up to think that we were at last looked upon as something more than beer-spillers and field-spoilers. Our attitude since that happy experience has been one of manly restraint and cheerful heroism.

The four days on the road were all very much alike—hard work and short halts—and the billets at night were pretty satisfactory on the whole. The men were generally put into barns or empty stables, while we went to cottages near by.

Well, by degrees we worked our passage to Rugby, the only town of any size on our way being Leicester, where the streets were lined with kind (?) souls who gave the men cigarettes and oranges as they marched through. Although I suppose these attentions were well meant they didn't improve the appearance of the march-past.

At South Wigston (two miles out of Leicester), where we were billeted one night, the Scouts took

charge of matters and made themselves very
popular by doing all sorts of odd jobs for us. At
this stage we thought our trials were over, as we
had only two short marches of eight and nine miles
to bring us to Rugby. Picture our misery, then,
when we were told on falling in next morning that
the whole seventeen miles were to be done that
day! This was the fourth day and many of our
feet were well worn owing to the heavy packs. As
it happened, I wasn't a bit sore, although I look
like this when fully loaded—

(There are a whole lot of things like revolvers
and field-glasses that you can't see in the illus-
tration !)

We set off singing, however, and kept up our
spirits the whole time, although it turned out to be
twenty miles. Our last halt was just outside Lord

John Sanger's house, and the grounds in front were filled with strange beasts, chiefly kangaroos. Much excitement was caused by these, and the following heated argument (which sounds like fiction) I actually heard :

1st Tommy.   See—yon's a kangaroo !

2nd Tommy.   Weer ?

1st Tommy.   Yon gray thing wot's 'opping.

2nd Tommy.   Geroot !   Yon's not a kangaroo. Yon's a —— 'ippipotimus !

Well, all our wanderings came to an end at last, and we entrained at Rugby for the South.

We're now in huts in a huge clearing in a pine forest—a great improvement on Lincolnshire.   It feels much warmer and the men all like the place, so our work should be easier now.   Even if it rains (as it hasn't done, where we've been, for ten days now) it won't be as bad as Belton, as the ground here is all sand. We really might be away in the wilds of Canada to judge by the views we get, and the smell of the pines is simply topping.

We've no definite news about leaving for the Front, but I don't think we'll be long here, as they're finishing the bath-rooms in the officers' lines and it would be too good to be true if they had been ready while we were still here to use them !

P.S.—Marching through Grantham, one of the men promised to bring back a *parrot* for a lady friend ! Just a sample of the optimistic imagination of Kitchener's Army !

CHAPTER VII

MANŒUVRES

CHAPTER VII

THE BELTON BULLDOGS—*Continued.*

MANŒUVRES

Witley Camp,
Godalming,
April 18*th*, 1915.

OF course one can always start with the weather, which is always with us and which for our first week here has treated us thoroughly well. The two long field days we had on Monday and Tuesday have left most of us alcoholically red in the face, and the men all look as fit as well-varnished fiddles. And still the weather goes on doing it.

Tuesday's manœuvres were on a scale as yet never approached. The whole division (twelve battalions, 15,000 men) was out for blood, and divided up into two hostile armies. It appeared that *our* army was following up a retreat of the " enemy," and that our battalion was " in support " —that is to say, not in the firing line, but close

E   49

behind, to be called on if needed. If you come to think of it, it would be rather pleasing if these little matters could always be arranged to suit us on active service. However, we set out with the intention of giving the said retreating enemy something to retreat for. Each side had its full complement of artillery, engineers, etc.

As things turned out, the action was what I suppose the real thing must be very much like. At any rate it was more realistic than usual. So this report may be taken as what a subaltern sees of an engagement.

The general situation was roughly explained to us (the officers) by the C.O. in a small wood by the wayside, we following his directions on our maps. Then we explained the idea in less flowery language to our N.C.O.'s, and they passed as much as they thought right on to the men. Thus, the C.O.'s remark : " The enemy must be actively engaged at this point," reaches Private Jones as : " You've got ter make 'em b——y well 'op it 'ere ! "

Then came hours of marching along dusty roads, which might have been the country lanes about Neuve Chapelle—only the cottages had their roofs on and the kiddies were playing in the orchards. Every few minutes we halt (no one knows why, as we are near the rear of the column) and get smothered in the dust of the motor-cycle dispatch-riders who keep up the communication with our advance guard. Then comes a halt by the edge of a pine wood and an order to " clear the road." A moment later the signal section of the Engineers come by at the gallop, a huge drum of telegraph wire unrolling from a limber and being laid by the roadside. This means that our artillery is somewhere near, and that they are laying the field telephone by which the observer will keep the infantry in touch with the batteries. As you can see, if this was not done the infantry might advance right under the fire of their own guns.

So the engagement must be beginning, though *we* know nothing of the position of the enemy yet. All we can do is to wait under the shadow the pines cast across the dusty road, and wait, while the motor cycles roar by.

This waiting is trying to the patience, and the men are getting restive when—*boom !* away in the far distance. The enemy's artillery has opened fire from the hills in front of us. A moment later our guns reply from the rear of the wood and the game has begun.

An order comes down the lines to advance, and

we turn off the road into the front edge of the wood. Here an engineer officer is busy with a little machine which buzzes in long and short beats with a quiet little noise like a blue-bottle on a window. This is the field telephone, which will report our advance to the gunners.

In the shadow of the wood we wait until, far ahead, a burst of rifle-fire rings out. Our men have got in touch with the enemy then. "Artillery formation on numbers thirteen and fifteen!" says our company commander, and we leave the cool wood for the blazing sun on the heather beyond, in small compact groups—

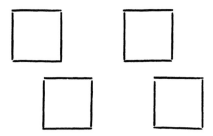

Each of these four is one platoon, which it is difficult for the enemy's guns to get the range on.

For a mile of boggy heath we advance in this formation until a message to reinforce comes back from the firing line. So we extend into the long line, which it is so difficult to injure with rifle-fire.

Right away to the horizon are lines of men, each looking like a moving fence. Every now and then each line disappears, as the men drop into the heather to fire.

As our line reaches the crest of the last ridge the sound of cheering and the flash of a line of bayonets in the sun announce the cheerful fact that the enemy is in full retreat before our first line's charge.

A little later the order comes to re-form, and we march home to eat almost indecently large dinners, and anxious to try our luck on a less mythical and elusive foe !

P.S.—I should have written more, but the lights all through the camp have been turned out. Expecting a raid ! Hooray !

CHAPTER VIII

DEUS EX MACHINA. THE SPIRIT OF THE REPAIR
SHOPS

.

CHAPTER VIII

THE BELTON BULLDOGS—*Continued*

DEUS EX MACHINA. THE SPIRIT OF THE REPAIR
SHOPS

May 2nd, 1915.

(By " Our Special Correspondent.")

LIKE the startled trout which, after a few frenzied
darts about the pool, plunges beneath some protecting rock, so our taxi (containing Owen Good-
body and myself), having flashed hither and thither
among the turmoil of London's " mammoth din
city," turned, breathless, through a tall gateway
and came to rest in an oasis of silence.

On all sides the high grey walls spoke of rest, rest,
rest, and peace for a time from the maelstrom without. Less, far less, is this a temporary home for
the broken, the ailing, than it is a haven prepared
for the weary who seek escape from the storms of
life. The atmosphere of repose, won for it by the

long years, hangs over this place as over a sanctuary. But now . . . A new spirit has entered the gates of " Guy's," a spirit which, though leaving behind her many an unnamed terror, cannot shake off *all* the dust from her feet as she enters even these hallowed precincts.

Follow this young officer as he moves, silent save for the light clicking of spurs, along the muffled corridors and up the long flights of stairs. Somewhere within these walls his friend, but yesterday so full of effervescent life and energy, lies, broken at his country's call. (N.B.—What about this for up-to-date journalism ?)

Almost one hesitates to break in upon the sacred moment of reunion. Surely the presence of a third person will be a profanation of the scene when friend, snatched from the very clutch of Death, meets friend. So we hang back here and watch from without.

A curtain is drawn back from a cubicle and shows a mere boy propped against a white background of pillows, a book on the mound of counterpane before him and a cigarette poised on its way to his mouth.

" Hullo, old chap ! How goes it ? "

(Our fears of profanation dissolve before this gust of British bonhomie.)

" Oh, I'm fine ! But whoever expected to see
you here ! " comes back from the pillows.

" You're not badly smashed up, are you ? "

" No, only a bit of shell in my leg. Got it there
yet. Sit down and talk. Take a cigarette.
You've got to stay a long time. By gum ! but I'm
glad to see you ! "

And then, the flood-gates being thus opened,
there follows a torrent of pure and undisguised
" shop talk," the subaltern just entering the Great
War game suggesting points, and the veteran (by
some stretch of elastic belief one *might* estimate his
years to have reached nineteen), the man who had
seen and done things, expounding Life and Death
as they appeared to him.

" It was on the Yser that I got knocked out. The
sort of thing they do there is to point on the map
and say : ' The Germans are *here* and *here*.
You'll attack their left flank. Now *go !* ' And
that's all the orders you get. We were on that
kind of game and they were dropping shrapnel all
round us. Beastly stuff. Our Captain got knocked
out and the other fellows. Then I got one in the
leg. That was on Monday. By Thursday I was
here."

Soon the talk necessitates reference to a map.

Covered by a newspaper on the chair by the bed is a heap of very muddy and tattered clothes.

" Just fish out my tunic," says the boy, " and I'll show you where we were."

The tunic is—almost literally—unearthed, and its owner feels in the various pockets. Before the required map is found, a strange collection has accumulated on the counterpane : little scraps of dull metal ; a pot bulldog with " Ethel " scrawled on it in pencil (" I mustn't lose my mascot ! ") ; and a small pocket-book (" That's my old platoon roll. Poor beggars—not many left now ! ") At last the map comes to light and is spread out.

" There's ' Plug Street,' and our line runs from there to the north. If you go to Plug Street or ' St. Ives,' give them my love. Oh ! that reminds me of a story . . ."

And so the talk goes on, while the neighbouring cubicles hum with similar subdued voices and visitors move quietly between the rows of beds.

Everywhere a spirit of cheeriness has pervaded the hospital-scented air—a spirit imported from the muddy flats and dark trenches of Flanders.

" Our doctor was awfully funny while he was patching me up. I laughed so much that he had to start all over again, once ! "

The bed still bears its miscellaneous burden of odds and ends, and both the patient and his visitors are absorbed in the examination of a small scrap of German shell (" which tore my tunic, but didn't hurt me ") when a lady steps into the cubicle and enquires how the sufferer is getting on.   Cigarettes are removed and the visiting subaltern stands up. No, he isn't wounded, only paying a call, he explains.   The new arrival chats pleasantly with the patient for a few moments, wishes him the best of speedy recoveries, moves on to the next bed and out of sight.

" Wonder who that is ?   Some ' Society for Cheering Wounded Tommies ' sends them round, I believe.   Seem to know her face, though.   No, she's not been here before."

" Oh, never mind *her !*   You were telling us about those German ' dum-dum ' bullets."

" Yes ; when they plunged them at us first time I was in an awful funk !   I felt myself all over to see if I wasn't hit.   Horrid feeling !   And it's quite true about those poisonous gases too.   I got a whiff of 'em myself.   Have another cigarette ?   Hullo ! What's the matter with that chap over there ? "

Something certainly seemed to be bothering the occupant of the bed on the opposite side of the ward, but, as his suffering takes the form of wild facial contortions only, it is difficult to gather his meaning. Realising this himself, he sends an emissary in a dressing-gown, one arm in a sling, and the mystery is solved—solved in a somewhat startling way.

" Do you know who *that* was ? " says the messenger.

" Who *what* was ? "

" The lady who came through just now."

" No ; who was she ? "

The messenger bends over the bed—the occupant of the opposite cubicle watching the scene with a wild joy—and whispers : " *The Queen !* "

The boy in the bed stares blankly. " Good Lord ! " he gasps, " I wonder what I said to her ! "

" And the man who walked through just before she came was the King ? "

The patient gurgles incoherently, then wildly seizes a cigarette, lights it and puffs furiously. " *My* hat ! And we all ought to have bowed and walked about backwards or something—oughtn't we ? But, I say, she's a real good sort, isn't she ? "

.   .   .   .

" You'll soon wish you were jolly well back ! But you *do* have some sport ! "

The visitors are saying good-bye now, and this is their parting message from the pale young warrior on the bed. But the voice is that of the Man-who-has-done-things, and the words are of the spirit of his kind. Tales of Death he has in plenty, glimpses of nameless horrors he can give one, but these, though they must for ever be with him, sleeping and waking, have no power to slay the spirit of obstinate and unquenchable cheeriness which is the spirit of Guy's, " The Repair Shop."

(N.B.—I'm afraid the " journalism " breaks down at some points, and the style shows want of practice. But—the fact remains that I have spoken to the Queen and *you haven't !*)

CHAPTER IX

THE MORALE OF OUR TROOPS

CHAPTER IX

THE BELTON BULLDOGS—*Continued*

THE MORALE OF OUR TROOPS

Witley Camp,
May 9th, 1915.

FOR precisely four months past it has been thrust
before us at every possible and impossible oppor-
tunity that our embarkation for that vague and
wonderful place " the Front " (where, we are told,
some war or other is proceeding) is absolutely im-
minent. The Padre makes it the subject of encouraging discourses. " In a few weeks, my
brothers," he says, " nay, in a few days——" We
encourage our blasé platoons with promises of
speedy departure. We ourselves buy large stocks
of meat lozenges and valises—for which we defer
payment, in hopes—— But nothing happens.
The same routine continues. No glad tidings
grace the company notice-boards. " The *Lusitania*
was yesterday torpedoed and sunk. Companies

will parade at the Q.M. stores to draw bootlaces at 7.15 a.m." we read. And private John Jones, who dashed to the local recruiting office on August 4th last, vaguely wonders whether he is the same person who was then so filled with Imperial enthusiasm—and if so, how much it must have cost to get himself into that condition.

Not that life is allowed to become too tame. We have the usual energetic field days to keep us from getting too lazy.

For instance, we left camp on Monday last at 9 a.m., rushed about in the sun till 9 p.m., took a wink of sleep under the stars and a thin blanket, started off again at 5 a.m., and finally reached camp at 8 p.m. on Tuesday evening. You can't get absolutely torpid on an outing like that.

One relieving feature of the jaunt was that we met Lord Kitchener, out to see how the New Army was getting on. No hints, unfortunately, could be gathered from his demeanour, the fact that he burst into ribald laughter when our company hove in sight being taken by some as a sign of pleasure and by others as merely derision. He gave no date for our departure, however.

Wednesday afternoon, by the kind permission of the G.O.C.—who probably either feared a mutiny or needed a day in bed—was set aside for battalion sports. As sports, these were quite mediocre, but a delicately humorous flavour was given to the proceedings by the sudden advent of a clown, a tramp, a nigger-minstrel, and a comic policeman. These, with the help of buckets of water, whitewash-brushes and a broken-down bicycle, raised the standard of public spirits to something almost approaching hilarity.

But these side-shows and special indulgences from headquarters are becoming strangely frequent, and from this it would seem that the authorities realise that, while others are doing the work, Tommy's patience, unless thus stimulated, must soon be exhausted.

CHAPTER X

SAM

CHAPTER X

THE BELTON BULLDOGS—*Continued*

SAM

June 13th, 1915.

HE attached himself to the battalion (in a purely unofficial sense) on a night when a select party, organised and directed by Privates Potter and Mackie, met in the pine wood west of the camp to discuss a home-made roulette board by the light of a candle. His official appointment to the influential position he occupied later is really the subject of this story.

It is popularly supposed that the glimmer of the candle, at a time and place where no candle should be, roused his curiosity, though Mackie half believes to this day that a furtive interest in roulette attracted him to the group. All that is certain is that, hearing a rustle among the twigs at his side, " Ginger " Mackie stretched his hand to grasp a warm bundle of feathers which by the

light of the candle proved to be as handsome a
little owlet as ever got itself into trouble through
inquisitiveness.

Ginger, whose mind was of the slow-moving type,
considered his captive from perhaps eight separate
points of view, and then, as he felt his hand sharply
nipped by a hard beak, pronounced his verdict.

" Young hawk," he said slowly.

" Nobby " Potter, who, by keeping a white
kitten and two frogs (the latter now deceased), had
established a reputation as a naturalist, treated his
friend to a pitying glance.

" 'Awk be blowed ! " he said, " that's a owlet,
that is."

Ginger mused a while. " I copped 'im wiv me
'and," he murmured, " and I'm goin' to keep 'im."

" You ain't got no place for 'im," said the group ;
" 'e'll die. 'E'll peck 'oles in yer. 'E'll crow all
night and keep yer awake. And 'e'll stink
'orrid ! "

" I'm goin' to call 'im Sam," said Ginger.

And that is how " Sam " enlisted.

Ginger Mackie and Nobby Potter joined His
Majesty's Army on the same day last fateful
August, and had since worked their way through the
vicissitudes of a soldier's life side by side.   Where

wit was needed, there Nobby steered their course; where muscle might avail, Ginger took command. But a time came when the eternal law of mind's superiority over muscle asserted itself, and a lance-stripe descended upon Potter, rendering him, for the whole of the first afternoon on which he wore it, godlike and exalted above measure.

Said Ginger, stretched to his full six feet three inches on the sun-browned moss of the hillside: " An' what about *me* ? " A cryptic remark which carried worlds of meaning, however, to his quick-witted companion.

" Well, 'ang it, I ain't a field-marshal—yet," said Nobby, " and as such I'm still allowed to converse—in moderation—with privates. Don't see why this 'ere stripe " (he regarded it lovingly) " should make any difference, Ginger."

" You'll get ikier and ikier till you busts ! " Ginger neatly avoided a clod of turf, turned on his side and fell asleep.

Though Ginger's prophecy came very far short of the truth, indeed there were elements of certainty about it, for a newly-made lance-corporal must perforce adopt that attitude which the unwise call " stand-offishness," and the discerning recognise as authority. Whichever party Ginger may in his inmost heart have belonged to, he chose, in public, to side with the former, and may be accordingly numbered with the unwise. Moreover, as this type of gentleman makes the life of his superiors unnecessarily arduous, a very decided coolness grew between Potter and Mackie. And the climax introduces us once more to " Sam," the owl.

Sam had, for some weeks now, been living on the fat of the land and at the expense of the Government, in a wired-in soap-box between the beds of Ginger and Nobby. Since his *début* he had grown, and was now almost a full-sized owl. His captor's affection for him had increased in proportion, and the two, strangely alike in many ways, would commune together on hot afternoons after parade, now and again sharing a biscuit or a piece of cheese. And when Ginger's grievance came into being it is not unlikely that he discussed it with Sam.

At last came a night, a desperate, fateful night, when the situation developed into open rupture between Ginger Mackie, private, and Nobby Potter, lance-corporal.

It was an indifferently-kept rule in the barrack-room that after " Lights out " there should be no smoking, and it was every N.C.O.'s duty to see that this regulation was adhered to ; so that when Lance-Corporal Potter found his room-mate and erstwhile friend Mackie puffing contentedly at a large pipe between the blankets, his duty was clear. But a voice within warned him that here must vanish for ever the last shreds of a friendship which once he had valued highly. The line of least resistance was easy, but Nobby thought of his stripe, and——

" Put that pipe out, Mackie ! "

A grunt from the blankets and an insolent puff of smoke were the only answers.

Let us draw a veil over the sad spectacle of a ten-months'-old friendship in its death-throes. Ten minutes later silence reigned in the barrack-room and the floor by Ginger's bed was strewn with the fragments of a well-coloured clay pipe.

Now that pipe was more than a mere favourite ; it was a fetish. Close examination of it, when it was less disconnected than at present, would have revealed an image of no less a person than Lord Kitchener himself. The rim of the bowl was formed by the great man's cap, so that when in full blast the pipe gave the impression that his lord-ship's mental equipment was leaking heavenwards in blue rings. Not a pipe, in short, to be lightly handled, and involving almost high treason in breaking.

So Ginger lay still by the ruins, fuming and, as quickly as his slow brain would allow, planning vengeance. He would show them that they had a man to deal with who would take no such insults as this. Life among these bullies was becoming intolerable. The world was peopled with tyrants. But he was more than a match for them, individually or collectively. Not another minute would he remain under the iron heel which had crushed him into the dust. Moreover they had smashed his pipe!

Slowly a definite plan formed itself, and Ginger raised himself on his elbow. Except for the hard breathing of its occupants the room was quiet, and the time seemed ripe. Stealthily collecting his clothes, Mackie crept to the door, opened it, and was gone !

The night was cloudy, so that the business of dodging the guard was no very difficult one, and ten minutes sufficed to put Ginger on the high road which wound between the black pines towards the land of freedom where a man could call his soul his own and not merely hold it on sufferance at the bid of lance-corporals.

At the end of the fifth mile Ginger sat down to rest. A faint grey veil in the east suggested dawn, and a sleepy bird above his head began to tune up his welcome of the sun.

Sitting among the pine-needles, his back against a tree, Ginger reviewed the situation for the twentieth time. He recalled the first clumsy recruit-days spent with Nobby, their walks together, their adventures and their games. The recollection of the latter brought back a vague sense of loss not felt before. What was missing? Ginger turned the question over in his mind, then: "By gum! What about *Sam?*"

This was serious. Sam, the comforter of his misery, the sharer of his sorrows, would certainly fall a victim to the tender mercies of the tyrants who had driven forth his master. Yes, undoubtedly they would "take it out of" Sam, poor unprotected Sam, now that his defender was gone. Sam was a good sort, too, who didn't talk too much. Action must be taken in the matter of Sam.

A workman, early abroad, swung round the corner of the road. "What's the time, matey?" asked Ginger.

"Three o'clock, or thereabouts," came the reply.

Ginger rose from the soft turf and turned towards camp once more, where lay the den of despots, the lair of inquisitors, and—Sam. Reveille was not till 5.30 ; he had plenty of time to slip in, liberate Sam in his native woods, and get away again himself. A little more difficulty in dodging the sentries, perhaps, but—well, Sam must be saved.

.   .   .   .   .

Peace still reigned in the barrack-room when Ginger quietly opened the door and crept to his bed. Sam opened one eye and regarded him solemnly. Something white on his deserted blanket caught Ginger's eye, and he stooped to pick it up. It was a pipe, a gorgeous clay, fashioned in the image of His Majesty King George V., and round its stem was tied a scrap of paper. Ginger tore this off and read—

"DEAR OLD GINGER,—Sorry I smashed your pipe which I know you was fond of it so pleese take this one instead becose I havent got no grudge agenst you only I as to keep orders. Whats the good of having trubble now when weve been pals so long so pleese take this pipe from

"Yours NOBBY."

Ginger slipped the pipe into his pocket and looked down at his friend. He was fast asleep. So was every other man in the room. For once his slow mind grasped the situation in a flash. Nobby was right. Well, Nobby was always right, now he came to think of it—brains *will* tell, you know.

Five minutes later Ginger was sound asleep in his blanket.

Sam, the sole witness of these events, slowly closed his wise old eye—once. But he never told anyone.

G

CHAPTER XI

UNDER THE CIRCUMSTANCES

CHAPTER XI

The Belton Bulldogs—*Continued*

UNDER THE CIRCUMSTANCES

May 16th, 1915.

A MERELY superficial judgment would not encourage one to credit Thomas Atkins with any depth of spiritual fortitude or many apostolic attributes. As a matter of fact he combines the strongest points of such pillars of the Church as Saul of Tarsus (before and after conversion), Elijah the Prophet, Job, and the psalmist David (in the latter's lighter vein). Or called upon to play Noah, Jehu, or Ananias, neither is he found wanting.

In witness whereof—

King George, Lord Kitchener, the local correspondent of the *Godalming Gazette*, and the Clerk of the Weather, having laid their heads together, an enormous *affaire de guerre* was drawn up during last week. The slaughter was to be on an immense scale, two whole divisions, including infantry, cavalry, artillery, and my platoon being embroiled. The originators (I might have said perpetrators) of the scheme forgot nothing. They *wouldn't*, of course, for it was for their own amusement and they all intended to be there. As it turned out only the weather person showed any signs of being present, and we couldn't get his range for effective rifle fire . . . But I digress.

I think it was on Wednesday that, with light hearts and heavy packs, we took the road for " destination unknown." I may be wrong—much has happened since—but for sake of argument let us say it was Wednesday. Six a.m. Having been on urgent private affairs the previous evening I had had almost three hours' sleep. (But that is beside the point—it is the inspired fortitude of Thomas I want you to observe throughout this story.)

Six a.m. saw us (if it was looking the right way) winding over the moors on a cloudy, windy morning.

Said the company Sergeant-Major to me : " It's goin' to rain, sir. Me nose itches. Me nose always itches when it's goin' to rain, sir." Then he relapsed into silence again.

Twelve o'clock came, after six hours of weary

marching, and with it came the sun. Then up and quoth a corporal who had overheard the Sergeant-Major's remark :

" Sergeant-Major," said he, " I'd have your nose up before the Commandin' Horficer for making a frivolous complaint ! "

Strange how the minds of this brutal soldiery run upon their vocation. For instance : last Sunday on church parade, when a number of men, anxious to hasten proceedings, got half a paragraph ahead of the rest in reciting the Creed, an incompletely subdued voice rapped out : " *Mark time* with that there Creed, you in front ! " Another digression.

To return to my story. We found ourselves, at 3 p.m., in a field adjoining a large country house full of wounded from Flanders and elsewhere. One of these strayed to the railings which divided us, and for nearly an hour discoursed to a gaping mob of the Front, and all that moves there. Indeed, it was only when he had had his fill of cigarettes, oranges, and the like that it transpired from a casually dropped remark that he was one of ourselves, a Kitchener's Army man, who had been bitten by a horse at Aldershot a week before. The meeting then broke up in confusion.

Talking about horses : I have a Scotch corporal

in my platoon, the very scottiest Scot I ever met. He talks the real Highland brand of the language. Last Monday at kit inspection he was deficient of a mess-tin. " Where is it ? " I asked him. " It's nae guid ! " he said, " a mewl trode on't ! " More digressions.

The galaxy of talent before mentioned (Kitchener, the King, and the rest) had agreed that it would prove diverting if we were made to sleep in blankets under the stars (if any) ; so twelve hours from our *début* saw us arranging our mossy couches with one furtive eye on the sky, which had by this time clouded over again.

We turned in early, as our start on the morrow was timed for 5.30 a.m.

There was some discussion, at this point, as to whether those of us who had brought pyjamas should change into them or not. The pros and cons don't matter, but the result was that some of us did and others did not. Clarence, for instance, who was sleeping in a rabbit-hole on my left, wore his. I, on the other hand, only took off my tunic and outer garments. My last recollection is of hearing Clarence say " D——! " as a drop of rain (though the doctor, sleeping beyond him, called it " heavy dew ") hit him on the nose. . . .

I was awakened by being trodden upon by a baby elephant which slowly dissolved itself into one Private Turner, my servant, when I came to look more closely, my left eye out of the blanket. " Quarter to four, sir ! " (Just as if that were any reason for waking me instead of an excellent one for *not* doing so !) Slowly I put my head out and— " Fizzzz ! ! ! " a gust of rain hit me fair and square. Everything, from the transport mules to Private Turner, was dripping merrily, my blankets were soaking, and my luckless discarded tunic was a pulp by my side. Cursing my lot I looked around me and my gaze fell upon—Clarence !

Hastily I woke the others on my right and we scrambled into Burberrys and stood round the sleeping form in its pathetic pyjamas, surrounded by its every other garment—all sodden.

Then we woke Clarence.

A little healthy merriment at four o'clock on a rainy, cold morning is a useful start for the day, and, considering he was more than half-asleep, Clarence was wonderfully efficient in his summary of the situation. . . .

By five o'clock, after a breakfast of coffee, bread and jam and rain-water, we were ready to start. Our battalion, we were told, was to act as an outpost line.   To the mere civilian this may convey little, but how well we hardened veterans know the dread import of the outpost scheme.   Visions of standing still for hours on end in this ceaseless " heavy dew " (curse that doctor ! thank Heaven this will mean extra work for him later—atishoo !) floated before us on the miniature rivers which trickled all about.

And these visions fulfilled themselves very creditably.   My platoon lined a dripping hedge, lying in the long wet grass, not allowed, by regulations, to smoke, but still cheery.   Not one of us, by eight o'clock had so much as a dry stitch on us, and the wind was getting up—a cold, steady wind, which blew little rivers down our necks and under our caps.   No so-called waterproof ever invented could have kept us dry, and certainly neither Burberrys nor the Service overcoats made any effort to keep the icy-cold water out for more than ten minutes after we started.   The men's coats, indeed, seemed to soak it up like blotting-paper, and a friendly rivalry sprang up amongst them, with bets as to who was wettest.

Though plenty of humorous blasphemy drifted along our line I never heard one genuine " grouse " ; and when it came to a discussion of the future—

where we should spend the night, what we should do
to dry our things, whether anyone had any spare
clothes in his pack, and so forth—the whole business was discussed as a tactical problem and without malice.   It transpired that the only dry articles
of apparel any of us had were a pair of socks in one
of the men's packs, and these were unhesitatingly
offered to *me !*   (That's the sort of little thing that
makes all this beastly business worth while.   God
bless you, Thomas !)

For two and a half hours nothing happened but
rain.   Then, away on our right, we heard rifle fire.
A few minutes later our patrols announced that
they had encountered the enemy in a wood to our
front, and following this a signalling party wagged
a flag message to us to prepare for an attack from
the right flank.

The attack, when it came, was launched with a
vigour which would have been very commendable
on a hot day, but was quite comprehensible under
the existing conditions.   It amounted to a bayonet
charge over about 1,000 yards of open ground.
We held our fire for close range, and the umpire
arriving at this opportune moment the enemy were
put " out of action," and had to retire to their wood
again.   They left three prisoners, however, who

cursed their fate and went and sat under a hay-stack, where they took off their shirts and wrung them out.

After another hour of waiting, getting colder and wetter (if possible) every minute, my Sergeant asked me to let him take out a patrol to try and lure the enemy out. I gave him permission and, from what he told me afterwards, it appears that he and four men charged a company of the foe, captured a machine-gun, and sent the whole lot flying in hasty retreat.

It was now about one o'clock, and we had all decided that the idea of keeping us out in this climate any longer was too Hunnish to be possible in a civilised country ; so when the " Cease fire " sounded we were all quite prepared for the fifteen-mile march back to camp.

Even the absolutely matchless patience of Tommy underwent a severe strain when the order came that we were to go into billets for the night !

Billets ! You can picture the men contemplating a stone floor in a barn and (with luck) a bit of straw. No dry clothes, no means of drying eight hundred shirts, no proper cooking arrangements. . . .

> " Here we are, here we are, here we are again !
> Are we downhearted ?   NO !   Let 'em all come ! "

So sang Thomas as he marched barnwards in the rain. No foul language, no cursing of those responsible for the scheme.

> " Wet through we are, wet through we are,
> Wet through, we are wet through ! "

chants the cheerful soul, as the water squelches in his boots.

Well, as barns go, this particular barn which our company got wasn't a bad one, and—redeeming feature—it was piled high with straw.   I settled my platoon into one end of it and went off to see about some food for them.   Shrieks of laughter brought me back.

" Morris don't like the *rats*, sir," someone explains.

" Well, I've killed one as big as a 'orse just now, sir," says Morris.   " Great b——y big brute as long as meself, sir ! "

It certainly *was* a fair sized rodent, and we handed it on to B Company, explaining that it would do for rations for the morrow.   B Company thanked us for it but returned it.   (Whack !   It nearly got the Corporal in the eye.)

The farm people were tremendously helpful, and let us light a huge fire in the farmyard, so that, when I left the men half an hour later, there was at least some hope of drying a few things—*if* the rain stopped.

Having seen them settled in, and in view of the fact that unseemly-clad forms were frequent among the comforting dry straw (the *only* garment of some), I withdrew to try and find a fire and perhaps a coat to sit in while my own things dried.

Eight officers were billeted at that one small farmhouse, but the room we used had a big open fireplace, and there was plenty of wood to be had, so we soon got a roaring fire. Clad in all manner of weird clothes, from the farmer's Sunday trousers to his wife's long driving coat (*I* got that), we crouched round the hearth while our clothes steamed gaily on the fender.

All our blankets were wet, but we slept just as we were, on the floor, and had a very good night, too.

Next morning broke upon us with fresh woes in store. The A.S.C. waggons, taking it for granted that we should be making for camp the evening before, had gone there and left us foodless ! The nearest village rendered two tins of biscuits and not more, and we inwardly prayed that the men would not arise and destroy us when they heard of it. But, bless you, they took it like an everyday matter and set out for the fifteen-mile tramp, in wet clothes and a biting wind, nothing inside them and no hope of food for at least five hours, just as cheery as ever.

I understand Mr. Atkins' physical defects, and I've had some experience in encouraging him to look after his health, with the result that we have had no cases of illness on the strength of the little jaunt I've tried to describe ; but I don't *yet* understand his mind.   All I can say is that recent experience of him leaves me with the hazy impression that he is a great man and a living example of *mens sana in corpore sano*.   And when he gets busy in Flanders I pity the Germans—under the circumstances !

CHAPTER XII

'ORRORS !

CHAPTER XII

THE BELTON BULLDOGS—*Continued*

'ORRORS !

On board H.M. troopship *Aquitania*,
Bay of Biscay.
July 4th, 1915.

JUST as we shook off the dust of Belton Park (or
was it mud ?) from our weary feet once upon a
time, so, last Thursday, did we treat the sand of
Surrey. It would have been a " moving spectacle "
in every way, our marching out, but for two facts,
one being the darkness and the other the rain.
But many of the Bulldogs had fortified themselves
(it had been pay day !), and the general satisfaction
was summed up in the remark made to me on
parade by my own Scotch Corporal. He fell out of
the ranks, saluted solemnly, and said : " Sirrr !
Beggin' yere parrdon, but numberr Thairrteen
Platoon's the vairy finest set o' men that everr
tairned oot ! " (Which I am inclined to endorse.)
Then he fell in again.

Railway journeys are all very much alike, and nothing (including sleep) happened until we reached —well, where do you think ? Liverpool ! Here they had evidently heard of our coming, as they had prepared the biggest ship ever floated to take us to our destination. At the station and all the way to the docks the men had been frivolously profane, now they just gaped and became picturesquely blasphemous. She certainly *does* look an awe-inspiring sight from the quay, too, and the fittings are what might be expected of a boat built for trans-Atlantic service. Officers, N.C.O.'s, and men are quartered like dukes, and general satisfaction reigns.

As our starting-point wasn't revealed beforehand there were no tearful relatives to make the familiar scenes, so we were spared *that*, at any rate—except for one or two who found their way to the camp, and one . . .

It was on the dark, wet road to the village station, and the company had halted while the leading troops entrained. Through the wet mist a figure in rather draggled hat, and carrying a small baby, slowly wandered down the column. " Thirteen Platoon D Company ? " it inquired. I told her she had found what she wanted. " Tommy

Hall," was her reply—no more. Of course I told
Hall he could fall out of the ranks, and there, under
the shadow of the black hedge, the ex-coal-miner
bade his wife " farewell." There were none of the
melodramatic manifestations so dear to the work-
ing-classes ; just a strong arm that crept round her
shoulders, and a faint sob. They stood quietly
together for a moment or two—then we had to move
on again. Tommy Hall, who " fell in " with such
squarely-set shoulders, her silent tears still on your
cheek, I shall always have a soft place in my heart
for you !

But to return to the *Aquitania*. Though she
is supposed to be rushing troops out to the Front,
there is no unseemly haste about her until she sees
clear water before her, and it took twelve hours
after we and our baggage limbers had been pushed
aboard for her to make up her mind to move. All
Friday morning she lay out in the middle of the
Mersey, commanding a rather fine view of the
shipping, but making no progress worth men-
tioning.

It was quite worth while to climb to her top
deck, all among the four giant funnels up which
(except for the gradient !) any large motor-car
could easily be driven. Perhaps one might be

lucky enough to make friends with one of the ship's officers who would explain his instruments on the bridge, or the thousand and one marvellous inventions which bristled on every side. Thus I was introduced to a weird machine which listens to sounds at night through ears attached to the ship's sides below water. It can hear the throb of a steamer's screw or the bell of a vessel half a mile away. Then there is a wonderful apparatus for closing (from the bridge) a water-tight compartment or door in any part of the boat. Beside this is a collection of small tubes which, at intervals, the officer will sniff at. A fire in any part of the boat confesses itself by these pipes and can be flooded by simply connecting the pipe in question with a central switch, exactly as a telephone operator does.

It was from the bridge, too, that the mate pointed out a wrecked " tramp " steamer, her back broken, stranded on a sand reef. " A German submarine got six altogether, yesterday," he said. This was one of them. All had been " got " not far from the mouth of the Mersey. Then he was called away, as our guard of two torpedo-boat destroyers ranged alongside. These were to accompany us out of the " danger zone " and two more would pick us up to protect us into the Straits of Gibraltar.

Coming on deck after lunch, we found ourselves bowling along in the wake of our two sturdy little guardians, either of whom would be able to " spot " and account for a submarine, should one venture near our course. On our port lay the crippled " tramp "—an evidence of the late presence of the Huns, and beyond them, dim in the distance, the Welsh mountains where a year ago—— But never mind that. Both the grim sign of the present and the appealing shadows of the past fell behind us at last and we were forging through the smooth blue waters of the Irish Sea, which, with thoughtful encouragement to our expedition, re- mained calm until we turned in to sleep the sleep of safety—for were not our two solid little watch- dogs still grinding their way before us ?

I was awakened next morning by a flustered steward, who popped a white face into my cabin and said : " All hands on A and B decks at once, sir ! " My watch said 5.40, and I thought this seemed unnecessarily early, so without getting out of bed I asked what the trouble was. " Submarine just missed us with a torpedo." And he was gone to turn out the next man. The idea of seeing a submarine in action was rather too tempting, so I got up, slipped on a pair of canvas shoes and made towards the deck, bumping, on the way, into a figure of fun in which close scrutiny revealed our —— in pyjamas, a short overcoat, and no false teeth ! On deck the men were collecting, each with a life-belt and a cheery remark about the Huns who had got us up so early. There wasn't the least confusion, and the stewards *must* have blessed the fates that had spared them a crowd of squeaking women-folk ! All that was to be seen of the fight was a very dim curl of smoke over the horizon behind us.

What had happened was this. Our escort had taken us well outside what was believed the danger zone, and had then turned to go back. Twelve minutes later the man in the " crow's-nest " on the foremast sighted a periscope some four hundred yards to port, and at the same instant an officer at the stern saw a straight line of white foam lengthening towards the *Aquitania's* side. For some time she had been holding a zig-zag course, taking perhaps a quarter of a mile before turning in the new direction. As it happened, she was just preparing to turn at this fateful instant and the stern swung to one side to allow the torpedo to pass through the white wake not a dozen feet behind !

Then did those Huns curse themselves, and well they might, for our wireless was calling up the two torpedo-boat destroyers and we were zigzagging about in a way which made torpedoing almost impossible, at the same time putting blue water between us and our invisible friend at a surprising speed.

But the wily Hun was not overtaken by justice all at once. From details our wireless picked up later, he bagged a large cargo-boat before our torpedo-boat destroyers finally sunk him. Thus perished U38, and his epitaph must be : " He nearly won an Iron Cross—but missed it." And a miss is as good as a mile !

That parade lasted a full hour, as the authorities wanted to have us handy until all immediate danger was past. So we stood in straight rows on the decks, watching the waves and making primitive and personal remarks about our fellow-man's raiment.

Then a school of porpoises rolled by, and, said Private Smith : " See ! What's them b———y big fishes ? " The creatures leaped from the side of one wave into the flank of the next in short jumps.

" Why, they're *rabbits !* " said Private Jones in amazement.

At this point Private Robinson begged to be allowed to fall out. Probably his greenish hue was due to the rather unpleasant swell which was making itself felt. But Private Robinson was merely the first of many. When I called my platoon roll that afternoon (my Sergeant being laid aside temporarily) some seven stalwarts hiccoughed to my call !

Well, I'm all right so far, and a fairly smooth sea to-day has brought many of the sufferers on deck again. The sea has been empty all day, but we shall be at Gibraltar by midnight, and this letter will set out on its journey home from there.

It is simply fine to see these men, some of whom I expect had never really seen anything of the sea before, enjoying every minute of the day. Although I had (occasionally) seen the sea myself, the rest of this remark applies to me.

CHAPTER XIII

ON BOARD

.

CHAPTER XIII

THE BELTON BULLDOGS—*Continued*

ON BOARD

Off the North Coast of Africa.
Wednesday, July 6th, 1915.

SINCE writing to you the other day we have got well on towards our final destination (wherever this may be), and so far have escaped submarines.

Life, from a literary point of view, is rather tame on board this old tub, and I haven't enough " copy " to make a chapter of the " B. B.'s," so I am just sitting down after dinner, robed in a wrist-watch (it is somewhat sultry) to write an effortless and purely " small-talk " letter.

Apart from what little interest we can get out of sham " alarm " parades and physical drill, there is only one interesting thing to report on. This is our passing through the Straits of Gibraltar yesterday. This morning was very misty, unfortunately, but directly after breakfast land was visible through

109

the haze on both sides of us. It was strange to think that on our right (or, as we now call it, starboard. Swank !) was the really and truly coast of Africa, even though it was too misty to see much of the country. For perhaps an hour the clouds hung over the sea, and on either side all we could make out was a hilly outline. However, a wind was getting up and driving off the fog, and every moment showed us more and more details. We were nearer to the African coast than to the Spanish, and the hills seemed chiefly bare sand with an occasional rock sticking out and overhanging the shore. Every mile showed us steeper and more exciting hills, until just before Gibraltar was reported in sight the African side flourished out into pure and simple dream country. Well, anyway, I'd not often seen such landscape. It was something like this—

The sugar-loaf hill was simply weird, with little

trees growing all the way up it, and standing all
by itself.

Then, half an hour later, we just caught a sight of
the wonderful Rock of Gibraltar itself. As far as
I can remember it, it looked rather this shape—

I wish it had been less misty, as it must be a
wonderful sight on a fine day.   It made us all gape
even as it was.

Since then things have been very tame up to this
afternoon, when we ran for some time along the
African coast again, and saw Tunis and the long
range of high and steep mountains which face the
sea in the district. Funny little Moorish houses
and mosques are perched in among the rocks on the

mountain-sides, and all sorts of strange roads and tracks run along the sides of the hills. Here and there a rocky valley, looking like the part of the

Ye up-to-date Infantry Subaltern.

Miners' Path under Castle Crag, runs inland among the rocks which overhang it on each side. As it disappears into the depths of the mountains it makes one think of brigand caravans and pirates and all sorts of jolly things.

To lie in a deck chair and watch all these exciting things slide past is really quite enjoyable. We are all in shorts and helmets now and my knees are brick-red to-night! Well, I'll leave this letter undone, in case something turns up to-morrow, though I'm afraid we're too far south for Malta.

Later.—We passed north of Malta yesterday, but we were a long way out, and all that we could make out was a low-lying shore with hills behind and a town and harbour. To-day we have been running among rocky islands which turned a wonderful purple towards evening, and the day ended with a real Mediterranean sunset, which I can't attempt to describe. All day long the sea has been a deep, clear blue, except our wake, which is vivid emerald green edged with white foam. This evening the water went violet, shading off into misty blue below the islands on the horizon. Behind these islands the sky was a deep liquid red, shading upwards through orange into greeny-blue until it became transparent blue above us—but it's simply impossible to write any vague description of the colours.

Our voyage is nearly over, and we shall be back at work again in a few days. There are some more

I

troops coming to join us, and then—Heaven help the Turks !

More letters whenever I can get the chance, you bet !

CHAPTER XIV

GUNS

CHAPTER XIV

THE BELTON BULLDOGS—*Continued*

GUNS

Somewhere in Europe.
July 11*th*, 1915.

YES, we are actually within sound of them now. Exactly *where* we are is (as the heading of this letter implies) not to be disclosed, but it's not very far from our final destination. Saturday saw us, after an adventurous voyage, at rest in a wonderful natural harbour, full of war-ships of two nations and flanked on either side by camps on the shores of the horseshoe-shaped island. For a whole day we were allowed to lie in deck-chairs on the deck and watch the exciting shipping which passed in and out all day long. The deck was cool (ninety-four degrees in the shade), and the shore looked pretty hot, so of course those in authority got us ashore at the first possible moment.

So yesterday we (pause here—to kill a new and

horrible kind of ant) were all packed into boats
and hauled ashore, where we found much to amuse
and interest.   If the details of our surroundings
are not awfully full it is because (1) we mayn't tell
anything, (2) because I'm lying on the ground
writing this by the light of a candle shaded by a
coat hung over a pick-axe.   The men are in bed
and singing loud and clear, and the candle can't last
much longer, I fear.

The inhabitants of the island "entreat us
kindly" (Acts xxviii., 7-10), and sell us much
unripe fruit and weird cigarettes.   They cause
much surprise and amusement among the Bulldogs, who shout at them to make *quite* certain they
will understand their broad Yorkshire !   I visited
one of the three villages on the island this afternoon, taking with me a loaded revolver which,
though never used, made one feel safer, as the
heathen weren't very prepossessing, and the village
full of odd twists and corners where a felon might
spring upon the unwary traveller.   However, their
chief amusement seems to be sitting at small
tables under the village fig-tree and drinking
strange liquors, and this keeps them quiet.

One of them tried to sell a hen-bird to a Tommy
to-day.   After examining it for a few seconds

Thomas yelled (they always yell): " Why, I'll
bet that chicken's older than *you!* " As the old
man looked about seven hundred—'nuff said!
He also offered him two shillings if he'd throw his
donkey in!

This benighted land swarms with small grass-
hoppers and large locusts ("as big as b——y
blackbirds," as one of " us " said), lizards and
insects yet unclassified and of terrifying aspect.
My candle is attracting the latter in shoals and
they are running all over my bare knees (I'm back
in Scout uniform, hooray!), so I can only continue
at the risk of being eaten alive—a sickly end.
So, with the expectation of a chance to write more
to-morrow, I'll chuck it.

CHAPTER XV

EVANGELI

CHAPTER XV

THE BELTON BULLDOGS—*Continued*

EVANGELI

Same Island.
July 15*th*, 1915.

THE products of this isle are divisible into three
main heads : the Useful, the Picturesque, and the
Superfluous. The first class may be dismissed as
purely domestic and uninteresting, comprising such
commonplaces as lemons, rope, matches, etc. The
third section—five-inch centipedes, scorpions, and
mosquitoes, with their attendants, the hornet and
the tarantula—need not claim a very distinguished
place in this history. But the second—— One
might easily build a story out of the " Picturesques "
of the island, a story something like this (which is
true).

Lying in my sun-shelter, too hot to do anything
at all, I can see a row of native hawkers selling
" Usefuls " to the Tommies. Their right flank is
strongly occupied by old Xanti Portianos and his

nephew, Evangeli. Of Mr. X. Portianos I know
nothing, save that he is dressed in a fur cap, Eton
jacket, and exceedingly baggy knickerbockers of a
barbaric cut; but of his nephew I know much, for,
as far as difficulties of vocal expression would allow,
we exchanged ideas on men and matters last evening.   Naturally a small boy with a name like Evangeli and a face to match had a complete advantage
on   his   own   ground   against   a   commonplace
Britisher, but he came down to earth eventually
and we are now pals.   Twenty minutes of assistant
salesmanship has bored Evangeli exceedingly, and
he is now on the look-out for some diversion.
Naturally the diminutive donkey which is grazing
on   the   hillside   suggests   possibilities.   Evangeli
selects a long thistle and turns towards his patient
dumb friend.   He is going to feed him—a pretty
thought.   After the fatigues of carrying two heavy
panniers of lemons over the cruel, sun-baked hills
the worthy beast is to have this tit-bit as a reward
at the hands of the cherub-child.   But stay : if
the cherub-child's object is *really* that of feeding his
animal surely he is making for the wrong end.
Whack !—It was a spiky thistle, and it shot the
donkey away like a billiard ball from the cue.   In
two jumps Evangeli was on its back, side-saddle,

and drumming merrily on its ribs with two bare
brown heels. Twenty yards of mad shamble.
" Hi ! hi ! hi ! " yells the cherub-child to drum
accompaniment—and then Evangeli notices a
lizard among the rushes.

The instinct of the hunter, which is the world-
wide instinct of the boy, brings him down from the
donkey's back on to all fours in one motion—to
the intense relief of the donkey. Uncles, lemons,
and pack-beasts drift out of Evangeli's life for a
while and he is a hunter among tall jungle grass,
hot on the trail of a gigantic and terrible reptile.
Shoulders low to the ground, and the small hind-
part of him swaying from side to side like a stalking
cat, the cherub slowly advances a stealthy hand,
then a knee, then a hand again. The world is a
jungle and contains only himself and his prey.
Softly the Approaching Doom, clothed in blue
shirt and pink striped knickerbockers, draws
nearer and nearer to its victim. The small straw
hat is actually raised for the final imprisoning leap,
when—" Evangeli ! " Uncles *are* a nuisance !
Probably more lofty schemes have been brought
to nought, more visions dispelled, more trackless
jungles dissolved into nothingness by importunate
uncles than this world dreams of.

Evangeli returns to earth and the fearless hunter squats on his heels at his despotic relative's side to serve questionable drinks to thirsty Tommies just off parade.

And the hidden observer of the hunt shuts his eyes to see, alas ! only in such a vision as any uncle might dispel, other small forms which he loves, tracking in their own mystic jungles on the happy hills of Home.

CHAPTER XVI

A VILLAGE SCENE

CHAPTER XVI

THE BELTON BULLDOGS—*Continued*

A VILLAGE SCENE

The Market Square
(of a small village you won't find on the map).
July 20*th*, 1915.

I AM engaged in the very unexciting work of commanding a picket in one of the local villages. Let me explain. Myself, with twenty Tommies, have dragged our weary limbs from camp up into the hills, where no soldiers are allowed owing to the prevalence of bad cognac. Therefore it is necessary to patrol this part of the country and keep errant soldier-men from going astray. Our headquarters are in the village square, where I sit me down under the trees at a small table, and the Tommies in two parties slowly patrol the streets (such as they are) in search of wanderers from camp, and to the awe of the inhabitants.

K   129

Mine, therefore, is a somewhat lazy job and
leaves plenty of time for writing, so I have assailed
the village store, and after some rather elaborate
acting succeeded in dragging forth a bad pencil and
this paper. I also bought (for sixpence) twelve
biscuits, which I have shared among five of the most
entrancing small boys one could find outside the
angel choirs. Finally an ancient, of horrible and
menacing aspect, raised his voice and drove my
little party away, and I can't get them back, though
three biscuits are left. I shall have to finish these

myself, a solemn thought. These beastly foreigners
(Kaiser and such) seem set on stealing my boy
friends away from me.

Well, while daylight lasts, I'd better describe what I can see from here.

We are in a sort of irregular shaped courtyard, in the middle of which is a well. Occasionally a small infant, of either sex, will drag a donkey up to this well by a rope and whack it soundly while it drinks from the trough. Or perhaps a juvenile inhabitant will stagger up under the weight of a huge bucket and coil of rope, let the bucket down the main central well-hole, and haul it up with strong heaves of brown little arms. Then the infant will stagger away again over the cobbles and disappear up one of the little side-streets which run into the square. The " grown-ups " of the village appear to do no work at all. Most of them are now sitting round me drinking the local coffee. This is really wonderfully good stuff, and it is always served with a glass of water—the object of the latter being to make the tiny cupful go further, I suppose.

Perhaps I have wronged the grown-ups, for they are now beginning to drift in from the fields in ones and twos, generally accompanied by a small donkey on which a tiny son is perched. The saddle doesn't look as though it was made for comfort, being constructed of wood, padded underneath with skins. But the small sons are generally chirruping merrily, so I suppose their anatomy is made to match! All around this courtyard are picturesque houses of different kinds. The one just opposite me, for instance, where the village idiot is sitting, is a fairly modern stone-built shop, but of a style which these artistic folk would never allow to pass just as it is. So they have painted the shutters blue and white, and rigged up a sort of dummy veranda round, above the lower windows. All along this framework a vine is climbing, and one trailing branch is even trying to wander into the shop-door.

Next to this is a little low-tiled building, its roof overhanging the cobbled footpath below it. Under the shade of this overhanging roof (only it would be an insult to try to draw them in anything but colour) sit the fathers of the hamlet and the grand-fathers of the angel-children.

A short way down the unpaved street on the right is a tall white building looking like silver against the deep blue of the sky, and casting an ink-blue shadow across the sandy road. All the colours, which are wonderfully brilliant by sun-light, are toning down now, and the lights in some of the dingy windows are beginning to glow. Very soon it will be too dark to see to write.

The Tommies not on duty sit round puffing contentedly at their pipes under the old fig-tree with the stone seat round it. A party of small boys has collected round them, and the whole group looks very strange in these out-of-the-world surroundings. The corporal in charge is showing his rifle to two tiny creatures, neither of which could top the muzzle of it, and (this is true) his pay-ment for the lecture is : " Give us a kiss, kiddie ! " Probably there are little corporals at home.

An aged gentleman at the next table to mine has lit a hookah pipe and is bubbling away merrily. I suspect him of being a Turk, but possibly his fierce demeanour is due to the game of " tig " which has begun round the mulberry tree at the other corner of the square. Suddenly there is a general stir, as a blue waggon drawn by two small oxen finds its way (goodness knows how it negotiated the rocky streets leading up to here) into the square. Its driver is a picturesque and nut-brown giant, evidently fresh from the hills, and clothed in wonderful blue baggy breeches and skin leggings and shoes. (I'm sending a pair of these shoes home. They are made of cow-hide.) As he and his caravan disappear the last glimmer of daylight goes too, and I can't see to write any more.

P.S.—The crowd inside the café looked far too interesting to miss, so I have warned the corporal in charge that I have altered my headquarters and have moved into the bar.

Oh, if you could see your little son now you'd tremble, for I'm apparently in the midst of brigands of the deepest and most melodramatic dye! Honestly, when I look round the company I'm jolly glad I've got my revolver with me, well loaded. The most blood-thirsty looking bandit is just opposite me. If I can only draw him. He looks as if he'd murder anyone for twopence cash! Also he's drinking an unhealthy amount of some strange green compound. A venerable (and venomous) old gent on my left is drinking a horrible amount of coffee, and looks as if he's got a knife in his belt.

Everyone is typical of the brawny, swarthy, dirty cut-throat one would only expect to meet in the Spanish mountains. The headgear most favoured

seems to be a dirty spotted handkerchief which either goes under the chin, as above, or hangs down the back.

Seeing me filling my pipe a bandit of more than usually gruesome and forbidding aspect has left his game of cards and sprung at me, brandishing— a match. So they seem not only friendly, but polite ! Well, I think I've described the cheery crowd at sufficient length, so I'll chuck it.

But oh, what tales for the Scout camp-fires when I get home again !

CHAPTER XVII

AT THE BASE

CHAPTER XVII

THE BELTON BULLDOGS—*Continued*

AT THE BASE

Somewhere in Europe.
July 27th, 1915.

AFTER four weeks (or is it four months?) of weary waiting the glad cry arose this morning: "A mail! a mail!" Such rumours have been circulated by unscrupulous people before, however, and it wasn't until a bugler blew the "Letter" call that the Bulldogs were sufficiently convinced to cheer. Then—*what* a cheer!

Well, all the news from home is most cheering. The more letters we get the better, and I shall certainly be reading those from home that I got to-day time after time. Reading is rather a problem here; you see, we are at the "base" and waiting our turn for the trenches, so there's not much work to do and all day is at our disposal. A few brighter spirits brought novels with them, but these have circulated so freely that we have now all read every one of them. Then some of us have tried writing letters to ourselves, sealing them up and getting the postman-sergeant to bring them to us. This plan is quite a good one, and the letter comes as quite breezy reading if you let a day or two go by before having it delivered. " Your dear Uncle Sebastian has passed away and has left

One of Us as we are!

How it suits some of the Tommies!

you £30,000." " The new racing car which your brother-in-law has given you is going well," and so forth. Then there is the relaxation of reading (for censoring purposes) the letters of one's platoon. Of course it's not fair to give quotations, but some are very striking efforts, I can tell you ! Last, and least, there is the *Peninsular Press*, which, being for circulation amongst the troops actually engaged here, tells nothing whatever beyond the fact that there are rumours afloat that a war of some kind is in progress somewhere.

We have moved on from our old and original island and have landed (after twelve hours' torture on an ex-cattle steamer) at the military base, from which details are sent straight across to the fighting. Consequently there are some mixed troops here ; some waiting their turn, like ourselves, and others resting after a turn in the trenches.

A walk round the island is quite exciting. At one minute a group (or rabble) of the New Army

A Sikh.

will wander past one, shouting broad *Yorkshire* language at one another ; the next moment you come face to face with a huge, stern Sikh who salutes you solemnly, though his uniform causes some doubt as to whether he is quite properly dressed to be out of camp at all. These gentlemen wear a turban, a beard, and a shirt, but seemingly little else !

Then a brawny Highlander comes swinging along chatting with a jolly looking little Ghurka, all smiles and teeth. These are by far the smartest

A Gourkha

troops here and always look happy, even though they are just back after breaking the record for length of stay in the trenches. A week is generally enough for ordinary men, but these topping little chaps keep smiling after two months !

Then there are some Egyptian troops, whose chief use seems to be as road-makers.

In the harbour, just as at our last stopping-place, are all kinds of boats of every shape and size, from a Dreadnought to a waterplane. Far out at sea on our left we can hear a steady booming, and a two-mile walk will take one to the coast, where a couple of " monitors " can be seen deliberately dropping huge shells on to the enemy's positions. Through field-glasses the effect of this shell-fire can be seen, and the sight of a high explosive shell bursting isn't easily forgotten. Just a patch of the ground gets up in a lazy, bored kind of way and slowly stands on end like a gigantic poplar-tree. If it happens to have been covered with men—well, it takes them with it, and, as it gently subsides, drops them again in sections. For days and nights this steady bombardment has gone on, and it is said that the end of it will be the capture of a certain hill which will give us, more or less, the key to the situation. Afterwards the fighting will be less heavy and the end of this particular campaign not far away.

Everyone, officers and men, is eager to be in at it and is keeping cheery in spite of the heat and the new pest, *flies*—millions and millions of the little brutes.   But oh, my brothers (as our Padre would say), are we not reminded of those beautiful lines :

> Flies on the butter—(Not that we've seen butter for weeks.)
>   Flies on the jam,
> Flies on the bacon,
>   Flies on the ham ;
> Flies are buzzing round your head,
>   And in your nose and eyes ;
> But *we*'re all enjoying ourselves—(Fact !)
>   For we don't mind FLIES.

CHAPTER XVIII

PRIVATE JOBLIN

CHAPTER XVIII

THE BELTON BULLDOGS—*Continued*

PRIVATE JOBLIN

The same old Desert Island.
July 31*st*, 1915.

TEN, twenty or more years in one very restricted walk of life rather blunts the aptitude for shaking down to new conditions and accepting new modes and customs of life. Consequently many of the Bulldogs who, I suppose, had quite lost all ambition beyond the scope of the coal-mine or workshop, find it difficult to keep pace with the bioscopic changes we have gone through since landing on foreign shores.

So when, after three or four days of wide-eyed wonder on board the boat, Private Joblin, for instance, began to sing the hackneyed music-hall songs of yore, we realised that his mind was beginning to accept the new surroundings as unworthy of further distrust. Familiarity breeding contempt, in fact.

In the same way, the short trip from the troop-ship to the shore, being a new experience, shut him up like an oyster, and it took a further three days to get him alive again. Then into the letters passed on to us for censoring began to creep sentences which hadn't been used by his friends and relatives for generations. " Just a line hoping this finds you in Health as it leaves me in the Pink," of course, is too sacred ever to be omitted, but it now no longer forms the *pièce de résistance* of the letter. Even attempts at description of " the niggers " (" it would make you die to hear them talk ") are now and then made. Indeed, Private Joblin is once more blossoming out.

The apathetic way in which he drove two clumsy sticks into the ground and slung a blanket over them as a very poor protection from the sun would never have suggested possibilities such as have since revealed themselves in him. He would now show you with pride a dug-out cupboard lined with wood. " Yon side for me fags, and yon for me pipe and matches. I keeps me water-bottle in a 'ole to keep t' water cool." And over all a wonderful fly-scaring machine, a relic of the rag-and-bone man's windmill, buzzed merrily in the breeze.

Moreover, Private Joblins has caught a tortoise !

That such things should really live wild outside the Norfolk Market, too, was astonishing enough to restore him to his oysterlike state of awed silence for a few minutes before surprise found expression in humorous blasphemy. " 'Nother one for t' b——y mernadgery. What next ! ? Crickets as big as b——y blackbirds, an' lizards and wot-not. Ee ! we *does* get 'em ! "

Joblin was now getting humorous and therefore worth watching. Ten minutes later I found him with a corkscrew, making a neat little hole through that part of the creature's shell which is thin and flat, just over the tail.

" Goin' to tether the blighter so's 'e'll stay 'ere and eat flies and black-clocks, sir."

" What are you going to call him ? " I asked unwisely, for Private Joblin shut up in his old way and became a coal-miner again. However, I have since heard him speak of one " Bert " in terms of derision as an unsuccessful fly-catcher.

CHAPTER XIX

THE SAD STORY OF CAPTAIN BOGGLES' RETURN

CHAPTER XIX

THE BELTON BULLDOGS—*Continued*

THE SAD STORY OF CAPTAIN BOGGLES' RETURN

The Desert Island.
August 5th, 1915.

CAPTAIN HORATIO VINCENT BOGGLES arrived home from the Eastern Front, bringing with him a wound in the—well, at any rate, a wound received while turning round to make sure that his men were following him as he charged the Turkish position.

Mrs. H. V. Boggles was naturally very pleased to have her husband back, and Miss Mona Boggles (the Captain's spinster sister) shared her pleasure. But not for long. The gladness of reunion was turned to horror when Horatio Vincent got fairly going. For instance :

Boggles was given a very clean, comfortable, and soft feather bed fitted out with white sheets and real blankets. Also a pillow. Into this he was gently steered by his wife and sister and left there

with the assurance that he would have his breakfast
brought to him at 8.30 a.m. the following day.
Horatio Vincent appeared dazed, but was actually
showing signs of undressing (so they assure me)
when his female relations left him. From this
point onwards we may assume that force of habit
overtook the wretched man, and we shall observe
his downfall under its baneful influence.

At 5 a.m. Mrs. Boggles, waking and remember-
ing the glad fact that her dear husband had
returned from the Front and was even then gently
sleeping in the adjoining room, slipped quietly out
of bed and crept to his door. Peeping round the
corner she was horrified to see Boggles reclining on
the floor, his head supported by the upturned wash-
basin, and himself dressed only in a great-coat,
Balaklava helmet, and one sock! As she stood in
horror-stricken silence, gazing down at her eccentric
spouse, a tassel attached to her dressing-gown
girdle gently swung across his cheek. " D——n
and —— those —— ——s of centipedes ! "
muttered the gallant Captain ; then opening one
eye : " All right, Colour Sergeant, get the company on parade. I'll be along in a minute ! "

Mrs. Boggles fled in alarm to bed again and lay
shuddering while from the next room rose a series of

muffled grumblings. " D——n stuffy place this ! Can't sleep in a slimy heap of fluff like that—give *me* the floor ! " and so on.

Then apparently Horatio Vincent got up, for his startled wife heard water splashing wildly over the floor and walls, followed by a mighty crash as the basin sailed through the window glass and a voice roared : " Here's the bucket, Johnson, if you want it for making the tea ; I've finished washing ! "

As the day progressed the Captain evinced new and strange characteristics. At breakfast, for instance, he seized his plate of porridge with both hands, seated himself on the floor, his back against the wall, called : " Chuck us a spoon and pass the milk-tin, someone ! " and began to whistle ! Again, when offered perfectly good kidneys and bacon he refused them unless he could actually see the tin they had come out of. Indeed, Mrs. H. V. found it was impossible to feed him on anything untinned.

Inanely congratulating himself on the fact that there was " no parade," Boggles spent the day roaming about the garden, followed at a safe dis- tance by his wife and sister, who, at intervals, found him doing the strangest things. For ex- ample, he carried with him one of the blankets from his bed, together with a sponge, razor, towel, jug of water, and walking-stick. At intervals he would thrust the latter into the lawn, fling the blanket over it and proceed wildly to shave, crooning to himself the while. Then, though the Boggleses had a most comfortable drawing-room sofa, Horatio sought out for his after-dinner nap— the rockery! Towards evening he busied himself in collecting four old sardine-tins (he had refused all other food during the day), a crust of bread, some bacon-rind, and a handful of straw. These he wrapped up in a greasy newspaper and made a bonfire of, sitting in the smoke and sniffing. "Thinking of the camp ozone," he explained to his wife.

Possibly his strangest act was while he was collecting the bacon-rind. He found his way into the kitchen where Evangeline the maid was making bread. For a time he stood watching, and then, muttering: "Here, you! Break off, fall out, dismiss! Let *me* come. *I'll* show you how to make bread!" pushed the maid on one side, emptied the dough on to the floor, spat on his hands (I blush to write it!) and fell to work. "What bread wants," he said, "is a strong male hand—preferably dirty, if you're out for flavour!"

As Horatio had eaten *all* the sardines with his fingers and hadn't washed all day he probably achieved his end. His wife did not sample that particular baking, so we can get no accurate information.

Poor Mrs. Boggles ! she suffered severely for a few weeks, but constant care is winning the Captain back to civilisation, though much irreparable harm has been done. For instance, when the vicar, paying an afternoon call, dropped his cup in astonishment at seeing the Captain eat a whole cake in four bites and held in both hands, Boggles called him a " —— clumsy —— who would disgrace a —— monkey house with his ——, —— manners ! " Again, the doctor's wife simply got up and left the house when Boggles, having licked his fingers (it was again at afternoon tea) and wiped them on her skirt, passed her a lump of sugar by hand, with a warning that " she'd already had two cups more than her share of the tea."

Of course, when the war was finally over and all her neighbours' husbands and sons came home with much worse manners, Mrs. B. got her own back by taking the Captain out calling, and sniffing pointedly when her hostess's mankind outdid him in sheer savagery. It was a conquest for her when Major

Tiffin, for instance, upset the dinner table in a struggle with one of his guests for the last grape, and when Colonel Bolthead, after the joint had been removed, put his feet on the table and lit a pipe.

Horatio's language was perhaps the hardest nut to crack. For years he used to adhere to a selection of adjectives which few dictionaries supply definitions of; and he will, I honestly believe, go down to his grave using in any society whatever the term " B——y Turks."

CHAPTER XX

LOOSING THE DOGS OF WAR

CHAPTER XX

THE BELTON BULLDOGS—*Continued*

LOOSING THE DOGS OF WAR

August, 1915.

THE American gentleman who somehow insinuated himself into the motley crowd who lined the hillside by the pier at Imbros must have got some excellent moving pictures, for the scene was both an unusual and a picturesque one. Lying by the temporary landing-stage were half a dozen steam-driven " lighters," long black barges capable of carrying two hundred or more men, and, in the open blue water beyond, more of these lighters were plying backwards and forwards between the shore and the small fleet of torpedo destroyers lying half a mile away. As soon as one of the lighters was packed with khaki from the thick masses of men on the shore, it steamed away and its place was taken by a new one, on to which fresh lines of troops filed, till it too was packed to its full capacity. Then out it would puff, carrying a dense freight of singing Tommies, whose legs swung hazardously over the bulwarks and whose heels kicked time to their favourite song : " Are we downhearted ? No, not while Britannia rules the waves (*not* likely ! !) "

It was well on towards evening before the last load of Bulldogs was transferred to the boats, and, as if to wish us parting " Good luck," the sun went down into the most glorious of many wonderful sunsets we had seen during our stay at Imbros. Moreover, with the night came an army of clouds like a legion of angels to guard us from the eyes of our enemies. Then, as silently as their protecting wings were slowly spread over the deepening blue, so silently we began to move out of the harbour into the unknown.

Over the packed decks there hung a tense atmosphere of suppressed excitement, too full for spoken or musical comment, officers and men alike rearranging their respective outlooks upon life to suit the new conditions and the great adventures looming among the shadows ahead.

And so the night deepened and our world narrowed down to a vague circle of deep indigo sea in which we slid quietly forward, alone save for the occasional glimpse of a companion torpedo-boat slipping ghost-like out of the gloom for a moment, to be swallowed again in the darkness.

And now came a thrill. The sealed orders containing our programme for the coming landing were to be opened. Crowded round a map, we traced the proposed movements of the various regiments to be engaged, while our Adjutant read from the official memo. So now we knew our part in the game, how, when the ——s had landed two hours ahead of us and driven in the small evening picquet that was posted at the point selected for the landing, we—the Bulldogs—were to follow them up as reserves, making good the ground and ready to give support in case we were needed. There was a low hill to be taken, a gun to be silenced, a tract of plain to be crossed, and then we should meet the first prepared position and the first real engagement.

All this, supposing the aeroplanes had done their work of reconnaissance well and the information was accurate, seemed straightforward enough, and we were content to know that the night's work offered great hopes of a successful stroke.

And now on our starboard bow we could see flashes of heavy guns, spurts of yellow light on the flanks of the dim hills that had come into view, where shells were bursting, and an occasional glare as a star-shell hung like a lamp over the scene. This was " Anzac," where the Australians and New Zealanders were busily " making good," and we sailed past the busy scene which slid by like a view in a panorama, the battleships lying away off the shore, their searchlights throwing vivid beams on to the rugged cliffs, and their guns flinging the crashing shells against these stubborn defences, while nearer to us a glow of green and red lights showed the outline of a hospital ship against the darkness. And all along the foot of these cliffs the rattle of rifle-fire swept back and forth as the Turks were driven up the slopes.

What these plucky Colonials had done many weeks ago it was ours to do to-night; and second only to the confidence we felt in the support of the Navy was the satisfaction of knowing that some-where near us would be thousands of our cheery, fearless cousins from over the seas. Also it was " up to us " to do our part, for England's honour, as they had done theirs for her colonies.

And now, away forward, we could see dimly a headland running out into the sea, silent and deserted, and, to the imaginative Bulldog, wrapped in the black mystery ; for this was where *we* were to land. What was waiting for us ? What had the first landing party found ? You can picture us standing at the rail with our pulses doing tattoos as we strained our eyes into the darkness.

Slowly our boat comes to a stop, and the absence of the rushing waves under her bows leaves a silence that can be felt hanging over the waters of the little bay in which we find ourselves. Only away on our right comes the distant rattle of a volley and the dull boom of an occasional gun at Anzac.

So the Turkish picquet has been driven in by the ——s and the land is clear. A lighter glides alongside us out of the shadow of the beach, and as it draws near—*crack*, *crack*, *r-r-r-r-r-rattle*, *crack ! ! !* From among the black mounds inland a sharp crackling of rifles, and then silence again. As the echo dies away over the still water all our conjectures return. If the Turks are driven back, whose is this firing ? What's happening beyond there, among the shadows ? We are still asking ourselves these questions as the lighter carries us landwards and we step for the first time on to hostile ground.

Orders here have to be given quietly, and almost

in whispers we get the men into formation on the rough, pebbly beach.

Again that crackling fire, and—was that a distant cheer ?

We are all ashore now and the boats in the bay are mere brooding shadows on a stretch of dull grey, though the thought of their protecting guns is still with us as we lead a way over the gravel into the blackness beyond.   To meet—what ?

This darkness for which we were lately so thankful is rather eerie now.   It is difficult to make out more than the merest outlines of the low hills on our right.   Hullo ! who is this ?   A man coming from inland along our line.   Whispered questions and the reply :   " Wounded in the back."   So we are nearing the introduction we have all had in our minds so long—the introduction to war as it is.

As we push on, through sweet, sickly-smelling scrub now, the darkness in front takes the form of a peaked hill and we meet the first slopes of its flank. And then, to our straining ears, there comes a voice from the blackness on our right.   Almost inaudible at first, it swells up into a shrill, wordless whine, quavers for a moment and then dies again into silence.   Then again, " Ah-h-h-h-h-h . . ."   This time it halts and inflects as though trying to frame some word, then, almost as though it would sing a few quivering notes, it sinks down the scale into the night and the shadows again.

The Bulldogs have seen many grisly sights and heard many gruesome sounds, but I doubt if any of these will remain so vivid in their minds as that voice, coming through the darkness from the Thing lying mortally wounded there in the blackness of sickly-smelling scrub.

On the steeper slopes of the peaked hill our formation is altered to four long lines, one in front of another, and each man two paces from his neighbour (though they *will* bunch up for mutual comfort, and one is tempted to shout at times !)

Our front line has met something exciting now, and—" *spit, spit, whissss !* " a swarm of bullets rushes over our heads into the night. We scramble on among the rough stones of the hillside and find ourselves on the edge of a long, deep trench, where are lying discarded rifles — and their owners. A Bulldog, stumbling over a rifle-butt, tries to lift it out of his way so that he may jump across the trench, but it is firmly fixed, the bayonet end down among the shadows at the bottom of the trench. Not waiting to examine further, we hurry on.

The desultory rifle fire has ceased, but as we reach the hilltop a shell—our first—flutters over and bursts behind us, followed by another and another. But we are safe in a dip of the hill now, and there we stay until dawn brings with it more shells and an advance over two miles of open ground under shrapnel and rifle-fire into an engagement the details of which would form another chapter, though one which I, at any rate, shall never write.

Well, that's the story of how the Belton Bulldogs landed at Suvla Bay, and you who have since read in the papers how it was another regiment who encountered and captured the first Turkish trench, may say : " So you didn't *do* much in the landing, after all ! " Which, owing to the part we were called upon to play, is quite true. The sensational bayonet charge against two entrenched battalions of Turks (the " picquet " of which we were told) was carried out by the ——s, and all we can claim is the distinction of " inking in their figures " without a casualty.

But some of you who sit at home, away from all the bustle and excitement, who only, so to speak, hear the rifle-crackle and the shouting through the night, will know the trials that waiting and the apprehension of the unknown bring ; *you* will think less hardly of the Bulldogs. And they in grateful return will wish for you that your waiting may never be broken into by any such horror as the Voice from the Night which has left a lasting scar upon the memories of *that night*.

CHAPTER XXI

SNIPERS

CHAPTER XXI

THE BELTON BULLDOGS—*Continued*

SNIPERS

The Trenches.
August 13th, 1915.

YES, the Bulldogs have burst the leash and launched themselves upon the unspeakable Turk. The heading of this letter suggests all that one has read of the humdrum life of the trenches in France, but I can assure you that for the past week things have been pretty lively. This is the first day I have had a chance of sitting still to write letters, and it is a longed-for relief to squat in a dug-out and connect up with the home that we are here to defend, after chasing people through their own back-gardens at the bayonet point.

Without any attempt at the dramatic, I have lived for a week in a hell worse than anything ever written or spoken would possibly suggest. To

173

describe the smallest incident would be to ask you to go down into the pit too, the very last thing I could wish anyone I loved to do. That particular type of fool who harps upon the details of the horrors of war has never exaggerated—that is all I'll say about it.

Well, the Bulldogs are a little fewer in number, a little overawed, but infinitely philosophical about it all, and miraculously cheery, too. Someone has said that man often reaches his greatest and his basest simultaneously. That fits the Bulldogs. The baseness of all this affair is so obvious to everyone that I won't waste ink in moralising on it. The greatness comes out when Tommy, after restless days and sleepless nights in Hell, keeps as merry and optimistic as ever, and even when he has bits knocked off him lights his cigarette and cracks jokes with the stretcher-bearers.

Well, I hope we have done a little to show Mr. Turk that we're out to win; at any rate he isn't very much in evidence to-day, except that his "snipers" are all over the show. These gentlemen live in trees with sufficient food and ammunition to last them for a month, and take pot shots at anyone they can see. Fortunately they're mostly bad shots. Some are *women!* A rumour was

current this morning that these ladies wore no
clothes and painted themselves blue ! I doubt this,
however. It sounds like a rather rude ruse for
encouraging Thomas to capture them ! Those he
has caught were dressed.

Conditions not being altogether favourable for
letter-writing (our machine gun has just opened fire
fifteen feet away), I'll stop.

P.S.—Down the trench a voice comes stealing,
and the words of the song are—

> " Down in Turkey where the Turk
>   Sleeps all day and does no work;
>   The fellows at 'ome what love to shirk
>   Oughter be sent to Turkey."

Cheers, and may " The Day " be soon.

CHAPTER XXII

"THE VALLEY OF THE SHADOW"

CHAPTER XXII

THE BELTON BULLDOGS—*Continued*

"THE VALLEY OF THE SHADOW"

A Trench.
August 27th, 1915.

MY DEAREST MOTHER,

This is going to be a grubby scrawl, but as I have quite a free time ahead I hope it may be a long one. We're in a trench where there's not much fear of the Turks rushing us, and all we suffer from is snipers. They have got three of my poor chaps to-day (two of them only wounded, though), so the obvious thing to do is to " keep down " and write letters !

Let's try a new (and impressive) chapter of the " Bulldogs."

CHAPTER THE NEXT

THE VALLEY OF THE SHADOW

The small boy who used to try and say the twenty-third Psalm all in one breath never guessed

that he would ever experience what that " Valley "
really could be like ; but having spent two hours in
it last Saturday afternoon he's going to try and
describe his experiences.

You must try and imagine us (at about the time
many of your local " knuts " were leaving for the
cricket-ground or golf-links) squatting on our
haunches in a shallow and dusty trench, listening to
the most appalling uproar you could dream of.
Behind us our big guns are roaring, above us the
shells are tearing through the air, and in front of us,
all up the long valley ahead, the crash of their
bursting is simply deafening. Somewhere (all too
vaguely described to us) are three lines of Turkish
trenches which must be taken to-day. But the
valley is broad and thick with bushes, and the
enemy is cunning to conceal his position. No
matter ! this terrific bombardment will surely
overawe him and make our advance a simple
matter. So we sit and listen and wait for
the hour to come when we are due to hurl line
after line of British Tommies against those
trenches.

Can you picture the feelings of all of us as we
watch the minute-hand slowly creep towards
three ? Ten minutes only now. Now only seven.

And what of us all when that hand shall have touched the half-hour. . . ?

The dentist's grisly waiting-den, the ante-room to the operating theatre—these multiplied a thousand-fold in their dread anticipation.

And now the moment has come. A whistle sounds—a scramble over the trusty parapet we have learned to know as a shield for so many hours, and the valley is before us. " *Whiss! whissss!* " The air is full on every side with invisible death. " *Whisss! phutt!* " A bullet kicks up a little spray of dust from the dry grey earth underfoot, another and another to left and right. The sensation of terror is swallowed in an overwhelming conviction that the only possible course is *forward* —forward at any cost. That is what we have been telling ourselves all through the long waiting, and that is our only clear impression now. Forward— and we instinctively bend as one does to meet a hailstorm, and rush for it.

Beyond the rough ploughed ground over which we are advancing lies a low, thick belt of brambles and bushes. Here, for a time, we can lie under cover and regain our breath for a second rush. The man on my left stumbles and comes down with a crash and a groan. Only an instinctive catch of the breath and the old conviction—forward at all costs—swamps all other sensations.

Down we go behind the kindly shelter, and " *Whisss ! whisss !* " the bullets fly over us.

Telling the men to lie quiet, I crawl through the brush to try and find our direction for the next rush.

Satisfied of our direction once more, our line bursts through the bushes and rushes over the open for the next hedge.   A few piteous bundles behind us tell of our lessening strength—and now a new horror discloses itself.   " *Boom ! whirrrr—crash !* " On every side the ground is torn up by the heavy leaden pellets as the shrapnel bursts above us.   And to left and right of me fresh sounds break out— dreadful human sounds which I won't describe. " We can't stay here, boys ! "—it's extraordinary how calm one's voice sounds, though one has to gasp to get breath to speak—" prepare to rush ! Rush ! " and we're off again into the invisible blast of death.

Hotter than ever this time, but there's another friendly hedge ahead.   Strange how one notices details, too.   The straws that cover the hard, dry furrows, the broken rifle, carefully cleaned and oiled that morning, the old plough under the hedge where we throw ourselves down breathless. "*Boom—whirr—crash ! zzzzzrrrr ! !*" Sand, stones, earth fly in all directions through a yellow cloud of smoke ; that was high explosive, ten yards behind us !

Surely we must be near the first line of trenches now and that bayonet-charge which I have been dreading more than all. We were told it was only five hundred yards from our trench to the enemy's—and none of us realise that we have left that trench far on our right, from where the Turks are getting our lines *broadside on*, where a bullet can do double or treble work.

A fellow next to me raises a wounded arm for me to put on his " field-dressing," and as I tie the ends of the bandage, on my honour, I remember how many scouts I have taught to tie that knot in the old club-room at home !

Two more rushes over the open and I find only three of my men left to follow me. The others are not *all* hit, of course ; many have got isolated with other parties.

We are all wondering where on earth we are by now, as we've certainly advanced quite seven hundred yards, and no trench yet !

Finally a rush takes us into a long, narrow ditch where we are safe from the bullets and apparently unnoticed by the gunners. Here I tell the men to lie while I crawl along it and find some trace of our position. Ten yards along, the way is blocked by the body of a young officer—he looks not more than nineteen, and quite happy, for his work has been well done—and beyond him are some of our own men, waiting developments like ourselves. Among them, to my delight, I find our old Colonel, smoking a cigarette and mildly cursing the fact that he too is lost !

After a talk with him we decide to " dig in " and wait for reinforcements to come up ; so the men set to work busily with the entrenching tools they all carry, and soon we have a quite cosy little trench and are safe for the time being. Our only fear is that some Turk may have found the same refuge and come crawling down upon us. So I take a rifle and lie at the end of the line, ready for him when he comes. But he doesn't come—and neither do the reinforcements.

Dusk is falling and we are preparing to spend the night in our safe retreat when a rustling comes from up the ditch. I grip my rifle and prepare for action. The sound comes nearer and I challenge it. " Friend," comes the feeble reply, and down the trench there crawls what was once—only a few hours ago—a man, and now . . . It is hard to tell the poor fellow that I can do nothing for him, but he is beyond all help now and he knows it. A drink of water helps matters, and he lies back, as comfortable as I can make him, and asks quietly for a "Woodbine"! Oh, you splendid British Tommy—not even to be daunted by those hideous explosive bullets we all know so well by now—there *must* be some Power behind you that lends you who suffer courage, and we who have "come through" the conviction that such courage can only be on the side of right and justice.

As night falls it is decided that I should take a message back to the Brigadier to report where our party is dug in, so I slip my revolver into my pocket and set out. The fire has died down now and I'm lucky enough to get safely back to the old trench and deliver my message.

That's the whole story. What we gained and what we lost that day form no part of it—the papers will show all that some time.

When, next day, we gathered on the beach behind the hills (all who were left of us) and found letters from home waiting for us, I'm not going to deny that all the little home topics you sent me to read helped on a reaction which was bound to come, and that I cried over them like a great silly kid ! But a shamefaced comparison of notes later on revealed the surprising fact that I wasn't the only one.

Yours ever,

YERBURY.

CHAPTER XXIII

IN THE TRENCHES

CHAPTER XXIII

THE BELTON BULLDOGS—*Continued*

IN THE TRENCHES

A Trench.
August 26th, 1915.

MY DEAREST MOTHER,

This is going to be a rotten, scrappy letter, as I've lost practically *all* my belongings and this is the only paper I can raise. During a horrible business we had on Saturday I had to take a message for our old Colonel, and I took off my " pack " to make crawling easier. When I tried to get back the Turks had a machine gun playing merrily on the place I'd left the old man in, and it wasn't healthy, so my equipment (field-glasses, pipe and baccy too !) are now in the hands of the enemy. Fortunately the old man got

[The paper is three little sheets torn from some kind of Army notebook, with " Roll of, Rank and name, Regt. No." at top of each sheet, and ruled for figures.]

out of it all right. We lost all our officers but six that day, and I'm lucky, I suppose. Two-thirds of the battalion have " gone under," too, but the remainder keep cheery and we're off to occupy another line to-night, a fairly safe one, though. The parcel came on Sunday last, and was most welcome—especially the cigarettes. The baccy *looks* good, but not having a pipe—— Well, I'm doing my best to get one second-hand, a thing I wouldn't have done in civilised life. But we're getting absolutely savage about little domestic details now. The political situation (as reported here) looks as though we might be set free in a month or two now, and I must say I don't look forward to a winter here. The fighting where we are is more difficult than in most other quarters, and is nothing like the description you will have read of the trenches in France.

Instead of being " dug in " all the time (and so comparatively safe from high explosives) *we*'re doing our fighting over ploughed fields for the most part, and almost always in the open. Now that the battalion has been so cut up we are really going into trenches (for a rest), and so we shall be safe enough for a bit now.

All your news about Keswick and Derwentwater

was most refreshing.   Out beyond us is a range of
hills rather the shape of old Skiddaw, and I often
look at it and think of the lakes.   Unfortunately
they keep knocking bits off it, though, with high
explosives.   We're improving the trenches this
morning, and for an hour they wouldn't let us work
—shrapnel behind and in front, but not *quite* over
us.   As soon as the bombardment had stopped, up
came the C.O. and wanted to know what we'd been
doing, wasting our time !

We get mails quite often now, and I love reading
all the news from home.   I always feel that the
letters I have written since we came here are very
scrappy, and rather a " drop " from those I wrote
from the islands ; but really I can't go into details
about what we're doing here.   Once you get out of
the thick of it and get a chance to write, you don't
want to think and write about it all.   Some day I
may take the job on, but not now.   Anyway, I mean
to let people at home know what war *really* is, if
I'm lucky enough to get home.

We're all keeping fit and well, but the diet of
tinned beef and biscuits is getting monotonous, and
a favourite pastime is to talk over an imaginary
meal which (even if we *could* get it !) would make
us all ill.   The heat isn't so bad now, as the winds

have started, and occasionally we even get showers. Anyway, we're used to the sun by now.

Yours ever,

YERBURY.

CHAPTER XXIV

LETTER TO A BOY SCOUT AT HOME

CHAPTER XXIV

LETTER TO A BOY SCOUT AT HOME

MY DEAR " JONAH,"

Thanks very much for your last letter, which came amongst a huge batch of ten—all of which need answering. So if this letter isn't a very long one you'll understand.

I believe they have let you see some of my home letters, and you may have seen one about a big attack we were in on August 21. Well, during that show I had to do two bits of scouting work, and I thought it might interest you and the other Scouts to have an account of these. Only I must ask you not to think I'm writing this for " swank," but just as a report of my first piece of real serious scouting work with people's lives depending on it.

Promise you won't think I'm " bucking " about my adventures, or I shan't go on ! . . . All right, then, that's a promise !

Well, the first bit of scouting came about like this :

After setting out to drive some Turks from a trench which was hidden away in very " thick " country, a whole lot of us found ourselves absolutely lost.   As a matter of fact we had got into a position between a section of our own men and a trench full of Turks.   I think a plan of the ground may explain matters best.

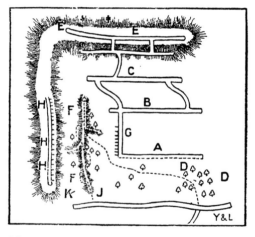

We set out from the point of our trench, marked Y and L on the plan, and were supposed to be making straight for the first Turkish trench

(A) in a triple row of trenches, all of which (A, B, and C) had to be taken.

We most of us lost our way (which was, of course, bad scouting) in the thicket (D), about one hundred yards in front of our trench, and somehow got going half left along the front of A trench.   (I have shown our advance by a dotted line.)

All this time Johnny Turk was blazing away with rifles and machine guns from the trenches, and also making himself very objectionable with a battery of artillery (shown ✠) behind Hill E.   Some of our men got into A trench and found it was only a dummy, about two feet deep, with no cover from fire, and simply an aiming mark for the Turkish guns.   I don't think more than half a dozen men ever got out of the trench again, the guns dropped so many shells into it.

We came in for our share, too, as we advanced over the ploughed fields looking for the Turks and getting more and more lost.

Finally, with exactly three of the half-company I started out with, I tumbled right into a little gully (F) where, after hunting about a bit, I found our old Colonel smoking a " Woodbine " and bandaging up the Adjutant, who had been slightly hit in the hand and neck.   I gave them some rum I had in my water-bottle, and we settled down to decide what to do. None of us knew where we were, and bullets were going over us *both ways*, which rather confused us. Of course these bullets were really coming from our own men in trench H on the hill on our left and the Turks in their trench (G) on our right.

Our final scheme was to dig ourselves in until dark and then find out where on the map we'd got to. The gully was full of dead and wounded, and not a bit pleasant, so before dark the Colonel decided to send a Scout out, first to find where we were and next to find the Brigadier and report our position to him. For some reason he fixed upon me. So, gripping my revolver with one hand and my courage with *both*, I set off.

I had a lot of difficulty in getting down the gully without hurting the poor fellows who were lying about in it, and at some places I had to get right out of it and trot along in the open ; but at any rate I found where we were, and put the " Old Man's " mind easy. Then I made for our old original trench (Y and L).

I knew by this time the rough direction in which it lay, but it was getting dusk, which made things more difficult. The people on Hill H were still firing wildly, except where in two or three places the shells had set fire to the thick bushes. The light from these fires not only made things look " creepy," but confused matters even more.

I seemed to be following that gully here and there for hours, and it was now getting so dark that I kept being challenged as a possible Turk. Also I should think I was asked fifty times to bring the stretcher-bearers to fifty different places, and fifty times I told the same lie, knowing well enough that no stretcher-bearers could be got out for hours yet, until the fire from the machine guns had died down, at any rate. Every time I got to a place where the gully was too full of wounded for me to pass, I thought to myself, " This is my last bit of scouting ! " but although I had to climb out into the bullets half a dozen times they didn't get me, somehow.

Finally a Tommy who really wanted to shoot me for a Turk pointed out the way to the trench, and I got over the parapet and into safety at the point J.

What happened after I had found the Brigadier and given my message I don't know, because I fell asleep on a pile of sandbags—or rather half of me was on these and the other half, including a pair of very dirty boots, was on another officer. I afterwards found he was a real live baronet, but that didn't make him any more lovable when he found me lying on him !

When I wanted to get back to the gully I'd left the Colonel in I found it wasn't healthy, owing to the Turks having taken over the far end of it. But I found the Colonel had retired to a point of safety not far from the thicket (D). Having rounded him up and piloted him to safety, I felt my scouting work was over.

But it wasn't.

The next bit of scouting came the following afternoon, when I got a message to say that there were still several parties of our men of various regiments " out in front," having been cut off and unable to get back to the Y and L trench on the previous day. One in particular of the —— Regiment was last seen without any officer, the major in charge having been killed about six hundred yards in front of the left of our line. And " the officer who brought the message from Col. ——— " was detailed to take a small patrol and go and bring this party in as soon as it was dark enough.

The first thing I did was to cut along and get up the hill into trench H, taking a good pair of

field-glasses with me.   I had to cut like a rabbit
over the open space (K), as the Turks had snipers
in most of the little trees scattered about.   Fortunately they were bad shots !   The trench H
commanded a very good view of the plain below,
and I searched it pretty thoroughly through the
glasses ; but although I could see where the course
of the battle had run by the absolute *mounds* of
dead, I couldn't see the party of ——s I was to
bring in.   In a dip in Hill E was what looked
like a whole battalion of Turks formed up, and it
was only by their stillness that you could tell it
was really the result of our bombardment with
naval guns the day before of a Turkish reserve
regiment.

There seemed nothing for it but to go out and
hunt up the missing party, as I couldn't spot them,
so I went back to the trench and got together the
best men I could find for my bit of scouting.   One
of them was an absolutely topping fellow (we'll
call him Johnson) who has since been recommended
for the D.C.M. for coolness under fire.

When it got dark my little party (there were
five of us) went along to the point J and climbed
out on our exploration.   The people we were to
find were somewhere out in front of that end of our

trench, and I chose that as being a good place, as I knew the ground there.

I'm not going to say I didn't feel funky, because we all did—except Johnson, who was simply in his element! But I only hope what I said to encourage the men didn't sound to them as hypocritical as it seemed to me! I tell you, Jonah, it was the " gobbiest " place I've ever been in—or ever want to be.

The moon was coming up, but the bottom of that awful gully was in shadow, so we stuck to it to avoid snipers. Now and then, for various reasons, we'd to climb out and go along in the open, and I can tell you we huddled down into every shadow we could find. We crept along as stealthily as burglars, me with my revolver cocked, and the men with fixed bayonets, and every now and then a spurt of flame and a " crack ! " from some bush or other showed us the Turks' snipers were still out. Otherwise the night was quite still.

Of course we kept down in the gully as far as possible and were safe enough there, except for the possibility of a party of Turks " on the loot " being amongst our poor chaps lying there in the darkness. And I don't know which was the worst—those who had been lying dead there all through the hot day, or those who gripped you suddenly by the foot and begged for water after their twenty-four hours out there. Either way it was rather a strain on one's nerves.

Suddenly Johnson said : " There they are ! " and was out across a field to our right before I could stop him. I looked out, and thought I could see someone moving, but couldn't be sure. We waited for Johnson to come back, but no sign of him appeared. Then came the most awful moment of all. Quite a series of cracking rifles rang out of the silence, a pause, and then a solitary voice called : " Help ! " from the direction where Johnson had gone. One of my party gasped : " They've got 'im ! " and I knew we all believed it, too. WELL, I couldn't go back and say that I'd lost one of my men, and I didn't relish the job of going out and getting attended to by the party of snipers who had got him ; but on the whole the second alternative seemed the less impossible, so I set out to find Johnson. Never have I been in such an absolutely *dripping* funk as I was out there in the moonlight, among the dark shadows of bushes and the huddled-up heaps left from yesterday's battle—and I don't mind confessing it ! The " voice " heard me coming, too, and kept calling " Help ! " but when

I got there I found (to my intense relief) that it was *not* Johnson, but a wounded man who had heard us moving about and thought we might be stretcher-bearers. I told him the old lie again and continued my search. After a fruitless ten minutes (which seemed ten hours) I got back into the gully and returned to my party. Johnson hadn't come in *yet !* So I prepared to make further explorations—when the man himself arrived with the missing party of the —— Regiment.

I could have kissed him, but restrained myself !

Our journey back was uneventful, and we got the ——s safely settled in the trench at last. Then one or two of us went out again to act as guides to parties of stretcher-bearers.

And that's just a plain account of the two most exciting bits of scouting I've ever done. I'm not superstitious, but I'll tell you for what it's worth that I carried the cigarette-case you Scouts gave me and the " Swastika " Thanks Badge that I got from the Hallam Scouts with me all the time. I guess these—or something else—kept the bullets off. What do you think ?

.   .   .   .   .

This has been a long letter, after all, and I'm afraid not half so exciting or interesting as a letter of this length *ought* to be, to justify its size.   Anyway, if you think they'd care to see it, please pass it on to any of my old Scout chums, with my best wishes to you and all of them.

Yours ever,

E. Y. P.

P.S.—I don't see any signs of this war coming to an end.   There *was* a time when I hoped we'd all be together again at Christmas, but I fear that's off.

P.P.S.—I hope the *Sale* will go off well !

CHAPTER XXV

JOHNNY TURK

CHAPTER XXV

THE BELTON BULLDOGS—*Continued*

JOHNNY TURK

Somewhere in Turkey.
September 9th, 1915.

I AM sitting on a rolled-up valise, a sort of hold-all in a dug-out on a hillside, while a weary " fatigue " party is digging more dug-outs. Writing isn't easy, as I have to balance the paper on my knee, so pardon ! This little hole in Europe (*i.e.* this dug-out) appears to belong to a Second-Lieutenant Huggins—at least, that's the name of the valise—and taken all round it is quite a good hole to live in. Our life has become analogous to the life of a rabbit, and we vie with each other as to the security of our respective burrows against the little attentions paid us daily by the Turkish gunners. Mr. Huggins, so far as security goes, has done well, as his lair is dug some

P .

209

five feet deep and strongly built up with stone parapets. Lying at the bottom he (or the present occupier, E. Y. P.) would be fairly safe against either shrapnel or high explosive. But when he lays him down to sleep I guess Huggins will be one of the sickest soldiers on the Peninsula, for in the left-hand a party of some 1,000,000 ants are at this moment digging themselves in ! Itchi koo ! as the song says.

We are really reserve, resting at present, but it seems that we have to do all the dirty work for the fellows who have taken over our nice comfortable trenches, and we shan't be sorry to get back into them on Sunday next.

The great advantage of our present position is that the hill we are on runs down to the sea, and every day we can get a dip, so long as we stay here. After a week or two in the trenches we certainly *need* plenty of bathing; and I caught two of the minor horrors of war in my shirt yesterday. One of them (the hen-bird) won the prize offered by one of the subalterns for the biggest caught. Private Jones's boast that he had caught one " as big as a mule " failed to materialise when the time for weighing-in came. So mine (no larger than an average mouse) won easily.

At this point I will break off for a lunch of bully and biscuits.

.   .   .   .   .

To resume, having finished my lunch, using Mr. Huggins' valise as a table.

Away to the east, along this ridge of hills, somebody is firing machine-guns and artillery, but as I can only see the smoke of the shrapnel away up in the sky above the hilltops, I don't know whether they are our guns or Johnny Turk's. If they are his we shall soon have some over us here, as he has picked up the Hun's habit of having at least one daily " hate." Another shell has burst—nearer us this time. Yes, Johnny is out for blood, so I have moved the Huggins bundle and settled myself on the hard, cold floor of the Palace Huggins, where the shrapnel bullets will have more difficulty in finding me.

The system the gunners go on is to send an officer up a hill to a place where he can see the countryside. He observes through the 'scope where the places are that the enemy troops mostly use, paths, wells, dug-outs, etc., and marks them on his map, probably numbering them points 1, 2, 3, and

so on.   He also has an accurate range-finder and a
telephone connecting him with the battery of guns.
If he sees a party of men at a certain spot, he wires
down :   " Give 'em socks at point 17," or words to
that effect, and we get a few shells along, while the
observing officer scores the hits.   Other days I
rather suspect he puts all the numbers into a hat
and shakes them up.   Then he picks one out, and
with luck the shell falls two miles away from
anyone and wipes out an ant-hill with great
slaughter.

He's a peculiar gentleman, old man Turk.   One
night when I was going my rounds in the trenches I
noticed a general hush at a point where generally
some of our liveliest boys want suppressing, so I
listened, as everyone else seemed to be doing, and
away from behind the Turks' trenches came a
sound of a band, playing some real racy oriental
music.   We had quite a promenade concert.
Coming from over the rugged top of a rocky hill and
through the quiet starlit night it was quite weird,
in a way, but we all enjoyed it.   In France the
Germans often have a bit of a concert before any
big attack, but although we thought Johnny Turk
might be going to do the same, no attack came off
that night.   We did have a mild attack once—see

enclosed account*—but the enemy never got within very exciting distance of the section of the trench I was responsible for. Anyway, you can show this printed account round, and tell everyone that your son helped General Maxwell to hold the Turks back. What! What!

Talking about generals : we all came out of the trenches feeling very sorry for ourselves when we were relieved a week ago. Certainly we were dog-tired and inexpressibly dirty. The day following our Divisional General elected to inspect us. Thought we to ourselves : " This means that he is going to see what is left of us, just to see if we are even good enough to go as a garrison to, say,

---

* **LOCAL NEWS**

Suvla Bay.

A sudden attack was made on the right of the 11th Division and upon the extreme left of the 29th Division about 2 o'clock on the night of the 1st instant. It commenced with shell, machine gun, and rifle fire on Jephson's post and along Keretch Tepe Sirt ridge. Brigadier-General Maxwell was holding the right section of the 11th Division when a body of the enemy attempted a bomb and bayonet assault under cover of their bombardment. There was no heart, however, in the attack, and it was easily repulsed with loss to the enemy.

The Navy, as usual on such occasions, were prompt with their assistance, and the flanking torpedo-boat destroyer with her searchlight lit up the northern slopes of Keretch Tepe and effectively stopped the enemy from pressing in along the coast.

Malta." Someone even whispered " India." Certainly no one would for one moment have suggested the possibility of our being of the *least* use as a fighting unit ever again. As a matter of fact, in numbers, health, and morale we were pretty weak. The General looked on the brighter side, however, and our dreams of Bombay were shattered pretty quickly. The General made a speech. He said that probably not since the days of the Peninsular War had troops such a hard time as we had during the past month. (We sighed solemn approval.) We had come through well. He told us that our hardships had apparently left us little the worse. (At this point a private fell forward in a faint—for which piece of acting I firmly believe he had been subsidised by his fellow-men ! The body having been ostentatiously removed, the General continued.) There were other hard times ahead for us, he said (exit dream of India), but for several days yet we should continue to rest. (" Fall in, those fifty men with picks and shovels ! " came the voice of a sergeant-major some distance away.) " And here y'are," concluded the General, looking round at the circle of faces ingrained with brown dust and looking swarthy in consequence, " here y'are all looking as fit as can be ! " He ended by

saying that when he had got our reinforcements out
from home he felt sure we should be as good a fighting force as ever—which I suppose we *shall* be. All
the same, we shall have earned a rest soon, I hope.

The ridge of hills we're on is very much the shape
(and nearly the height) of the Maiden Moor and
Catbells ridge. First comes a place like Eel Crags,
all covered with dug-outs on the Newlands side and
occupied by hundreds of troops. Then you come
on, still on the same side, by a foot-path to about
the middle of Maiden Moor. Here you will find *us*,
only instead of our homes looking down into the
valley, they look down on to the sea-shore and
away out to sea, where we can see one or two rocky
islands and far away the coast of the mainland of
Turkey, a bit of Bulgaria, and a bit of Greece.
Over on the other side we can see right away down
the Peninsula and pick out all the positions you
read about in the papers. Following on the ridge,
you come to a dip before reaching the hill corresponding to Catbells, and here is our trench,
running over the saddle of the hill. Beyond, on the
slope, is the Turkish trench, and somewhere about
where that old " skeleton " is that we used to see
from the lake as we rowed to Keswick, the Turks
have their guns. They also have one beyond the

end of the ridge, about where Crossthwaite is. Well, that gives you the general situation of our part of the line, without saying too much.

The trouble at present is that they can't locate the exact position of the Turks' big gun, which is very cleverly hidden. The Navy, the artillery, and the airmen have all been hunting for weeks, but so far none of them have put it out of action, and " Striking Jimmy," as we call him, goes on calmly dropping nine-inch high explosives about the hills. Fortunately he doesn't often hit anything really important (touch wood !—he's just sent a shell in our direction).

I met Owen quite unexpectedly on the beach the other day. His section is stationed some miles from here, so I shan't be likely to run across him again. It was very lucky seeing him at all. He was very busy making pumping arrangements for the water supply, and I (as usual, in charge of a fatigue-party) was asleep under one of his water-tanks, when he began to curse me for being on prohibited premises. It was quite funny ! Then he recognised me, and we had a whole afternoon together. He's had some pretty rough times and narrow escapes, just as I have, but we've both got so far and quite hope to finish all safe now.

Don't ask me how things are going here. You, who see the newspapers, know far more than we do.

CHAPTER XXVI

NIGHT IN NO MAN'S LAND

CHAPTER XXVI

The Belton Bulldogs—*Continued*

NIGHT IN NO MAN'S LAND

September 15th, 1915.

FROM the previous chapters of this narrative you will have gathered that the Bulldogs are fairly intelligent, fairly cheery, and (sometimes) fairly sentimental souls. Now I'm going to try and show you a new side of the breed and, incidentally, to " make yer flesh creep."

First of all I must briefly go over the geographical situation in which the cruel buffeting of fate and staff officers has landed us.

On the lines A, B, C is a very irregular-shaped trench occupied by rude and depraved British soldiery. Some hundreds of yards of rugged ground separate this line from the line D, E, F, held by Turkish gentry of no mean repute, and no manners whatever. To the *rear* of each of these lines is ground where Briton or Ottoman may disport himself at will—though at risk from stray bullets which may fly over his own trench from that of the enemy. But *between* these lines of trench is No Man's Land. Our people have taken it twice, and twice been shelled out again, and large patches of the thick scrub have been set on fire by shells and are now blackened wastes. Here and there strange shaped boulders crop up, but mostly all is thick, prickly scrub, from two to six feet high, rising and falling with the contours of the knolls and gullies. Altogether a happy-hunting-ground for snipers and an uninviting land for the Bulldog who values his skin. For all day long over this heath the bullets are whistling and kicking, varied by an occasional shell dropped in front of one or other of the opposing trenches.

If No Man's Land is unpromising by day, when it echoes to the rattle of the rifle and the buzz of the bullet, it is possibly even more sinister when, after nightfall, it becomes a silent and menacing sea of shadows, the haunt of the nightbird—seeking who knows what ?—and filled with vague rustlings now and then dispelled by the sharp roar of a chance shot which rattles and dies away among the echoes of the hills, to leave the land to sombre silence again.

And out into this eerie tract of lurking horrors it has been the lot of six of the Bulldogs, under the alleged "leadership" of the writer of these chronicles, to creep for the purpose of laying barbed-wire entanglements to hinder the progress of the agile Turk, should he be tempted to pay calls.

The scene when the seven apprehensive souls scaled the parapet and crawled quaking out into the night to mingle with the shapeless shadows ahead must have had its ludicrous side as well as its obviously painful one. And the contrast to the scene when a gilded and well-fed staff officer airily gave the luckless seven their orders (" You'll just go out and lay barbed wire about. A hundred and fifty yards away will be enough. Fine day, isn't it? So long ! ") must certainly have been marked.

Said the officer (his courage forced into the top notch and strenuously held there) : " Come on, boys, we're quite safe here in the dark. Safe as in the trench. Dash you, Smith, don't make so much noise ! " (Nerves.) " Now follow me. You'll be all right ! "

Lifting each foot carefully like a stalking burglar the little party advanced with the stealth of Red Indians, making, if anything, slightly less noise than a herd of camels, and convinced that every step, as it crashed and echoed into the night, could be heard in every corner of the Peninsula.

A stray shot from the Turkish trench rang out. Private Smith dropped the coil of wire he was carrying, with a deafening rattle, and the party stood still and thought of their individual misdeeds, and the new lives they would lead if, by some miracle, the Turks omitted to turn all their machine guns on to them. Moment succeeded breathless moment, and no devastating blast of fire swept them to sudden doom. The officer, whose duty may be briefly summed up as being to fortify the men by feigning valour he didn't possess, gulped once, and by some superhuman agency got his rigid muscles into working order again. Had it been less inadvisable he would certainly have lit an airy cigarette. Quite the blasé veteran, the iron-nerved devil-may-care, and so forth. The night was fortunately dark, a merciful assistance to his pathetic stage-effects, but he had the grace to thank the gods who had made him something of an amateur actor.

" Hang it all," he said, carefully controlling his voice, " we'll never get any work done before daylight if you're going to panic every time a Turk sneezes! Come on!" And so the "wiring-party" found its way unharmed through the glowering shadows to the scene of its labours, led by probably the most shameless hypocrite in Europe.

Did I mention that the Brigade Staff had instructed the hapless officer to reconnoitre the ground *beyond* his line of entanglements in addition? Anyway, these were his orders, so having got his party working under the guidance of a sergeant whose genuine contempt for the darkness and all it harboured was only exceeded by his officer's assumed contempt of these matters, the latter wandered away toward the Turkish lines, taking with him an unwilling private soldier, chosen for his ability in controlling his feet. . . .

What they found of military value *you* must not be told, as the brigade were next day, in the report such as Casabianca, had he survived, might have written. And what they found of human interest is best known to the night-birds which flapped solemnly away at their approach. It is enough to say that the ramble was by no means a pleasant one.

But when, the wiring-party having been collected once more, complete, the explorers returned to the shelter of the friendly parapet, each of them

Q

swelled with a manly pride in dangerous work well done, and felt richer in confidence in his own nerves under new stresses. In short, all felt themselves not a little heroic, and it was not until daylight brought with it obvious consideration that the danger was really slight and that the work done was less than that carried through daily and nightly by a thousand of our fellow-men, that we came down to earth again, and, seeing things in their right proportion, vowed to continue our work that night with less melodrama, and to be *quite* frank in writing home upon what might have become a very richly-coloured topic.

CHAPTER XXVII

FRIVOLITIES

CHAPTER XXVII

THE BELTON BULLDOGS—*Continued*

FRIVOLITIES

September 19th, 1915.

THE feeling that we have overcome the first rude shock of modern warfare is a pleasant one, but has accompanying drawbacks. For instance, we realise that while such matters as large and intrusive shells, Turks, flies, bullets, and barbed-wire are merely the unavoidable incidentals of active service, some of the matters which at first we should have included under this heading are in reality avoidable. Petrified biscuits, for instance, a month ago were rocky slabs and nothing more. Jam was palpably the produce of the turnip-field and the treacle-well (I'm on delicate technical ground there—*does* treacle come out of a well, or was it the pure invention of *Alice's* Dormouse ?) Again, bully beef was a cold, suety compound of leathery fibres. Now we revel in luscious bully stews, flavoured with preserved vegetables—" Julienne "—and Oxo gravy, followed by a really delicious pudding which one would never suppose was really crumbled biscuits (yes, the same rocky slabs !) baked or fried in dripping and flavoured with the despised turnip jam ! These discoveries are merely the outcome of our desire to improve what originally appeared a hopeless state of affairs.   But, as I say, to realise that there may, after all, be better things leads to heart-searchings if carried too far.   The Bulldog, fed on some toothsome compound of biscuit and jam, may have vividly recalled to him happier days when puddings like these were matters of course, and more automatic in their appearance on the table.   All of which leads to reproachings and yearnings sore.   So when a memorandum arrived from Staff Headquarters telling us the glad news of an eagerly expected supply-ship, carrying eggs, biscuits, and a hundred other luxuries to make life worth living, we were not long in appointing an emissary to go down to the shore on our behalf.   Loaded with all available bullion the battalion could raise, and numerous cheques (in hopes), the chosen corporal set out.   In all he carried some fifteen pounds to be spent on such things as should seem to fill our most pressing needs. Moreover, he carried with him what proved to be of more worth than all—a sense of humour. This was his story on his return.

The quay, he told us, was literally packed with " tin hats " (staff officers) all scanning the horizon with expensive field-glasses and cursing the sloth of the promised supply-ship. Behind them, on the beach, a small army of orderlies waited to carry away the spoil. Our man, not to be outdone, pushed his way through to the front and viewed the harbour. Only the usual grey battleships and three destroyers with one small native sailing-boat were to be seen. No sign of the supply-ship yet.

For half an hour the party waited, clinking their money and furtively edging each other so as to get the best places. Then the Turks dropped a high explosive shell fifty yards away. But the gallant band stood their ground, fortified by the prospect of those eggs. An hour passed, and still no boat, no eggs—but plenty of shells. And curses.

And then up spoke a small voice from the tiny native sailing-boat, now beached a few yards away. " Leemonarde," it said, " vaire goood ! " For a moment the awful truth was hidden from the anxious and distinguished crowd on the quay. Then, like the bursting of a nine-inch shrapnel, it

dawned in all its horror. *This*, this leaky, creaky
Greek tub, this paintless, rotting wreck, *this* was
indeed the vaunted " supply-ship " ! ! True,
they fell upon it and made its owner's fortune in
less than five minutes, but the eggs were more in
the nature of relics than refreshments, and the
biscuits—we knew the brand too well before we
left the island !

So it was a dejected party which wound its way
back to the trenches that evening, to be met with
the jibes and revilings of its disappointed com-
panions, and pursued by the tireless voice : " Leemonarde—vaire goood ! Vaire goood ! " (Inspiration) : " *Rather* good leemonarde ! "

Anyone with sufficient enterprise to fit out and
float a genuine supply-ship, and who will take the
risks afforded by submarines, has a small but
certain fortune waiting here. Only don't offer
lemonade !

As I suggested at the beginning of this chapter,
we have to some extent recovered from the first
horror of all this sordid business, but judging from a
postcard I saw addressed to the brother of a
" casualty " by one of the poor fellow's friends,
some of the men seem to have reached an almost
enviable state of *sang-froid*. " Dear sir," it ran,

" sorry to tell you Pte. Blank was killed in action on the 18th we have divided the parcel you sent him amongst us kind regards."

That was all.

CHAPTER XXVIII

SHELLS

CHAPTER XXVIII

The Belton Bulldogs—*Continued*

SHELLS

September 23rd, 1915.

When you have lived for ten days in a region where they wander whistling overhead, where they somersault eccentrically in circles, where they drop bits of themselves with the buzz of a drunken bumble-bee, where, in fact, they do everything *but* burst, you come to know the projectile family fairly intimately. In fact, some poetically constructed Bulldog has christened the various members of the family.

First there is Whistling Willie, a bustling soul, who does his journey, between the boom of leaving his front door and the moment when he sneezes up a cloud of dust in front of our parapet, in about four and a half seconds. You can almost hear him saying to the Turkish gunners : " Now then, you chaps, come on, buck up, look alive ! That's it, off

287

we go, *booooom ! zizzzzz !*   Here we are—tishoo ! '
Yes, he's a brisk, pushing lad, is Willie, but rather
superficial really.   There's more swagger and dust
about him than the result justifies—although it's
only fair to say that he once threw up a stone large
enough to upset the Adjutant's tea.   Probably
the war will end (if ever) with that deed of
questionable military significance to his credit,
and no more.

Willie's cousin, Whispering Walter, also of Ottoman origin, is a fellow of infinitely more worth and
solidity.   Though he takes longer over his trip
from the muzzle to the mark he makes up for lost
time when he gets there.   It is rather as though he
gave his gunners instructions to push him off slowly
so as to give him time to pick a good place to drop.
" Very good," they say to him, " off yer goes ! "
Booooom !   A pause.   Then Walter comes into our
area—" *Whizzlizzlizzle*," he   whispers to himself
confidentially, as much as to say, " Now *where*,
down below, is a good fat Brigadier, or a mountain
battery, or a pile of stores (dash it, I must hurry
up and spot *something;* I'm nearly exhausted)—
oh, a girls' school, a cabbage-patch—anything ! "
And   down   he   comes—*whang !*—as   often   as   not
half a mile from anything he could damage.   **There**

is a lesson on the futility of procrastination in Walter's methods.

Walter has two brothers, Clanking Claud and Stumer Steve. Claud always sets out, like his elder brother, in a meditative mood. Having travelled a sufficient distance and found nothing worthy of his mettle, he decides, apparently, to show his independence by never coming down from his airy height to earth at all. So "*Kerlank!*" he says, and disappears ostentatiously in a cloud of white smoke some fifty yards above us. True, he showers down a lot of little leaden marbles, but that merely shows his spiteful nature.

And then there is poor Stumer Steve. "If ye have tears, prepare to shed them now," for Stephen is both blind and dumb. Though he sets out full as his brothers of resolution, though, like Walter, he whispers promises of daring deeds, like Claud, passes with discriminating deliberation over the ground below, yet his final descent is a hollow and meaningless affair, though pathetic withal, "*Plunk!*" In a word the requiem of Steve. A young and apparently vigorous life robbed of its final destiny, a career despoiled of its rightful goal. Often we find he is filled with—sawdust! Sawdust! Like any sixpence-halfpenny doll!

Sometimes he is empty altogether. Poor Steven, the best that can be said of him, even when in desperation he lands upon a stone and goes hurtling away in spiral somersaults, is—" stumer," and even *that's* an American word !

Quite another kettle of fish is Greasy Gregory. There is a solemnity, a grandeur, and a determination about Greg that inspires respect. Also he is just about twice the size of his fellows and takes quite twice as long in making his way to earth. The mysterious and rather awe-inspiring feature of his performance is that you never hear him start ! Possibly you are sitting over a slice of bacon or a savoury bully stew when he makes his advent known. Just a greasy flutter overhead and then " *Crash !* " Gregory has come.

Everything gets up and changes places in a cloud of yellow dust and smoke. The atmosphere being thick, things that have no sort of right there get into intimate and inconvenient places (tea-pots, tunic pockets, etc.), and I have spent as much as twenty minutes in a time of famine separating Gallipoli Peninsula from raspberry-jam after one of Gregory's little jokes.

Last, and least, comes the clown of the party— Airy Archibald. His speciality is aeroplanes, and his efforts are acknowledged to be purely humorous by both sides. His methods are something like this. On some still, cloudless afternoon a distant buzzing sound is heard, heralding the approach of an aeroplane. Instantly Archibald springs into life. *Whoop-pop !*

Somewhere (it generally takes a good deal of finding) a tiny puff of smoke appears against the blue. Never by any chance is it in the same quarter of the sky as the aircraft. *Whoop-pop ! Whoop-pop !* One after another they leap up to have a look. The airman never takes the smallest notice, but sails serenely on, and never yet have I seen Archibald get within a thousand yards of his object. Once, so rumour has it, he *did* get nearer, so near, in fact, that two of his bullets hit a wing of the machine. But the shock of success was too great, and Archie's empty shell falling to earth put two of his own gunners out of action ! This story I cannot vouch for, but this I know, that after a monoplane has actually disappeared over the horizon I have seen Archibald jump viciously at him four times and every time miss him by quite three miles ! Well, here's to you, my comic friend. You add a humour to life, and I wish the others could follow your lead, and, taking life less seriously, give us as wide a miss.

R

CHAPTER XXIX

KEY TO SKETCH

CHAPTER XXIX

THE BELTON BULLDOGS—*Continued*

KEY TO SKETCH

September 28th, 1915.

ATCHI BABA.—The hill over which all the trouble at the south of the Peninsula has been. Following on this line to the right you come to Cape Helles, where the original landings took place (not shown here).

ANZAC COVE.—Headquarters of the Australasians; all along the high ridge they have climbed up practically precipices and dug themselves in.

SUVLA BAY.—Landing-point shown and line of advance on Friday, August 6, and Saturday, August 7, dotted in. Between Lala Baba and Burnt Hill (where we found the Turks had lit the bushes to stop our advance) we got heavily shelled. Many of our wounded could not escape from the fire.

245

LALA BABA (now " Yorkshire Hill ") was taken on the night of our landing. We spent the night there and advanced over remainder of the single dotted line next day.

HILL "10."—The Turkish guns were here. We took a lot of ammunition here.

CHOCOLATE HILL.—Captured on Saturday night.

SCIMITAR HILL.—Scimitar Hill is now a maze of trenches facing Hill W.

HILL " W."—A strong Turkish position guarding Anafarta. We have tried to take this hill (see my letter describing an attack).

ANAFARTA.—A village which we *hoped* to get in the first rush, now partly in ruins owing to shells from our ships in the Bay. The ridge beyond is our objective so as to command the Narrows.

KARAKOL DAGH.—The range corresponding with Maiden Moor and Catbells (see previous letter). This sketch was made at a point corresponding to half-way up the Green Path above Manesty.

SULAJIK.—A farm where we got mixed up in a rather hot battle. More can be told about this after the war !

THE SALT LAKE.—Dry sand in summer. More than two men together crossing it get shelled. We have crossed it *as a battalion* twice ! All round

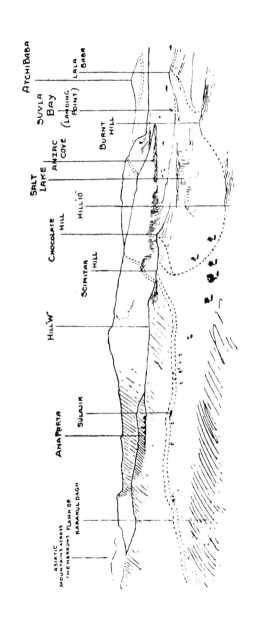

ATCHI BABA
LALA BABA
SUVLA BAY (LANDING POINT)
BURNT HILL
ANZAC COVE
SALT LAKE
HILL 10
CHOCOLATE HILL
SCIMITAR HILL
HILL "W"
SULAJIK
ANAFARTA
ASIATIC MOUNTAINS ACROSS THE NARROWS FLANK OF KARAKUL DAGH

the coast, along which we sailed before the landing (see my letter) are thousands of troops of all colours. also huge stores of food, etc.   In the higher cliffs by the shore are hundreds of dug-outs like sand-martins' holes or rabbit-warrens, as the Turks shell the whole beach-line regularly.   Troops come to these dug-outs after a spell in the trenches, to rest. We are no better than rabbits !

The Indian troops are between Chocolate Hill and Anzac, just right of the former.

Trench line (as at present) dotted in double.

This is, of course, only approximate.

CHAPTER XXX

"RERUM CAUSÆ"

CHAPTER XXX

THE BELTON BULLDOGS—*Continued*

" RERUM CAUSÆ "

(*A True Story*)

With rifle, hand-grenade, and gun
In France we chase the heinous Hun ;
But rifle, gun, or hand-grenade
Don't shift the Sultan's sons a shade ;
They hold their ground, and we, perplexed,
Consider what to give them next !
And while we sit in thought profound
They mine, and wire (*and* hold) their ground.
In fact it's only *by mistake*
      We ever make
      The faithful quake.

  e.g.—

As noted heretofore, in France
We lead the Teuton quite a dance ;
And rumour once, so rumour tells,
Was rumoured in the Dardanelles
That, what with rifle, bomb, and gun,
We'd fairly got them " on the run."
Field-Marshal Jones, on hearing this,
Said : " Here's a chance we mustn't miss ! "
Quoth General Jones, when told the news :
" Luck it behoves us not to lose !
Go with victorious roll of drums
(Before the contradiction comes)

And tell it o'er and o'er again
To raise the morale of the men ! "
And so, sonorously they hove
Their news abroad at Anzac Cove . . . .

From information it appears
That echoes of Colonial cheers
To Turkish lines were wafted back.
" Allah ! " they cried, " this means attack
Gird up your loins, Kismet hath cast ;
The Unbelievers come at last ! "
Then cartridges three thousand score
They banged away, and yelled for more ;
Bombs by the bushel crashed and cracked
In pyrotechnic cataract ;
While rockets swept the summer skies.
Nor lacked they bonfires—no, nor guys
(For well may Turks in aspect vie
With Fawkes of sacred memory !)
Nor was the conflict close confined
Nor uncontagiously inclined.
In less than seven minutes had
Three murd'rous miles of men gone mad,
All furiously letting fly
Without the vaguest notion why ! . . .

A midshipman upon his watch
Suspended sipping " Special Scotch,"
And stood astonished as he saw
Such sudden evidence of War ;
And then, in less than half a shake,
He had that battleship awake.
With whirring wires and blazing bells
He signals, " Load each gun with shells !
Fire and reload and fire again ! "
And so they work with might and main. . .

Among the hills our " Gunners " too
Had heard the horrid how-de-do,
And from his evening bowl of beer
Battles the burly bombardier.

Till suddenly throughout the dark
Is heard the busy batt'ry's bark,
And growl of gun and shriek of shell
Is added to the grand pell-mell.
Whizz, crack, and bang ; crash, whack, and boom,
Uproar enough to rend the tomb.
And all (I think I made it clear)
Caused by one patriotic cheer.
Two hours they carried on with zest,
And then . . . both sides retired to rest.

MORAL.

A moral lies beneath my lay,
But what it is I cannot say.

CHAPTER XXXI

IMAGINARY LETTER CENSORED BY E.Y.P.

CHAPTER XXXI

The Belton Bulldogs—*Continued*

IMAGINARY LETTER CENSORED BY E.Y.P.

The Dardanelles,
October 13th, 1915.

Shot & shell is flying over me as I write these few lines hoping this finds you as it leaves me at present in the pink. We cannot get no beer out here as there is no pubs & no houses—We are near the Sea so i can now get a Wash and also wash my Clothes. My shirt is full of —— (censored). So Dear Wife I think this is all this time so good night. dear wife give my love to my Sister-in-Law and our Ethel also our Joseph William & my Brother Judd. as he had is name took has he his the one has ought. Dear Wife the Butter you sent come undone—dear Wife you Better use 2 news papers instead of one next Time and string not Wool—Tishew paper his no good for lapping up things not Butter any way. So I must now conclude Dear Wife. Yours Truly   Walter.

s   257

CHAPTER XXXII

RUMOURS

CHAPTER XXXII

THE BELTON BULLDOGS—*Continued*

RUMOURS

October 13th, 1915.

WHAT with one thing and another, the average Bulldog's morale is getting badly strained. When you come to think of it, it has risen and fallen, and fallen and risen again (according to circumstances) with monotonous regularity for nine weeks now. Under fire, or in positions where, if the Turks knew of them, they certainly *would* be under fire, all the time. Now it is the news that two hundred thousand Turks are attacking our line two hundred yards away —and down goes our morale. Then comes the contradiction, coupled with a statement that we have taken Atchi Baba and seventy thousand prisoners, and up goes our morale again, only to fall with the next new thing in high explosives that drops delicately among us.

At first our skins were thick enough to withstand

rumours uncorroborated by something solid in the way of proof, but the constant wear and tear has left spots on us that are rather susceptible to highly coloured stories of things past, present, and future.

Some of these would, if repeated, lead me perilously near the brink of a series of libel actions, but two which have lent a flavour to life in the last few days may, I think, be safely exposed. The Press Bureau accepts no responsibility as to their truth or otherwise, however.

A sergeant—we will call him Joshua Jones—of the —— Regiment, was one day bathing in the limpid waters of Suvla Bay. It was a beautiful, warm summer morning, and Sergeant Jones had that particular portion of the bay all to himself (except for an occasional jelly-fish), as only the lower animals—Turks, jelly-fish, and the like—were yet abroad.

What was the Sergeant's astonishment when, swimming towards the shore, he observed a stranger awaiting him. To be exact, and to curtail the reader's suspense, a real live Turk was calmly sitting on the astonished soldier's pile of discarded garments, apparently cleaning his rifle.

Sergeant Jones's military mind grasped the situation in a flash. From a strategic point of view the enemy held the advantage (not to mention his opponent's personal effects), and seemed satisfied with the arrangement. The sole weapons on the side of the British force engaged were the stones on the beach and a strong right arm, and in that order he played his cards.

The second shot, catching the Turk, as it did, under the ear, drew his immediate attention away from the hostilities for a while and allowed the attacking force to gain a strong tactical position (*and* his trousers). This practically closed the engagement, and peace negotiations were entered upon at once.

" Wotcher doin' 'ere, eh ? "

" Engleesh ver' gooood !   German damrotten ! "

This, and the handing over of the rifle, practically constituted unconditional surrender, and Souliman Ali Bey was marched off to the nearest guardroom. All that he told our credulous staff later on, and all that they, believing it, passed on to us, is it not written in the Book of the Archives of the ——th Division ?   But, believe you me, it was *some* rumour.

Shem El Pot Ali was another Turkish gentleman captured under very similar conditions, but it is more with regard to the story he . . . (deleted by

Censor) that I have to write. For, according to him, the Ottoman Army is not only in a sorry plight, but has been actually *promised* peace by the 18th of this month, so that it is of little use our troubling to attack them. The 18th inst., according to Pot Ali, is the date of the great religious festival of " The Most Honourable and Serious Untailing of the Imperial Pig." After the 18th the Turkish Army will either be withdrawn altogether or so " fed up " that it will be no use attacking them, for they wouldn't fight if we did. " Thus," says Pot Ali, " it were better that no attack be made whatsoever." Selah !

One other rumour, the choicest of all, and widely credited throughout our brigade. We are detailed to sail for India on the 21st inst. to relieve some bloodthirsty Territorials who are pining to come over here to fight. It is absolutely settled !

The misguided officer who told me that the same rumour was rife among his regiment at Helles last May (they are *still* at Helles) is a kill-joy and a spoil-sport of the worst brand, whose sole aim seems to be to ruin the Bulldog's morale by causing it to perform gymnastics—now up, now down again.

CHAPTER XXXIII

"DE NOCTE IN FOSSA"

CHAPTER XXXIII

The Belton Bulldogs—*Continued*

"DE NOCTE IN FOSSA"

October 23rd 1915.

Down the steep hillside, like the path a raindrop finds for itself over a window-pane, a brown scar wriggled amongst the olive-green scrub. From the low ground by the sea its course could be followed from where, on the skyline, the irregular drab line seemed a meaningless twist of loose soil, to where it took the form of a dark crack in the flank of the hill, a black ribbon flanked with a wall of sandbags, and finally down and down until it towered its seven feet of depth to shut out the view on either side completely. This was the Ditch. . . .

Cut deep into the steep side of a " nullah " well in rear of the trench, a large square " dug-out " held a small but eminently select party of sub-alterns at dinner. The table was a sugar-box raised on none too steady legs, the chairs had begun life as

ammunition cases, and the meal itself was born of
tin in various and motley forms. Tin is the bulwark which holds back the waves of starvation on
active service, but the cunning of man has devised
almost infinite possibilities round which this
bulwark may be built.   For instance :

" Fresh ' spuds,' by gum ! " mumbled Dicky
Dooley through an Active Service mouthful.

" Wrong again, Dicky, they're desiccated. I
saw Parker opening 'em this morning. By the
way, we've begged the tin for a seat in our dug-out,
as soon as it's empty."

" Well, I must say you do things in style," said
Dooley.   " Seats, by gum ! There's only room for
me in my burrow.   Have to put my boots outside if
I want to take 'em off at night.   And where did
you and Mac get your timber from for that fancy
roof you've rigged ? "

" Where *did* we get it, Mac ? "   Anderson looked
over the table to where McKie was busy with a
fork amongst his plate of stew.   " Think we ought
to tell him ? "

" I'll jolly well pinch the whole lot of it while
you're asleep to-night if you *don't !* " threatened
Dooley solemnly.

" Well, if you want to know, Anderson and I

palled up with that little engineer officer who keeps knocking about. *I* admired those absolutely potty bridge traverses he's putting up, and Andy asked him in to tea."

" We gave him marmalade and buttered toast," said Anderson, " and he wrote us out a chit for the wood."

" But not until we opened the last cake," added McKie ; " that's what absolutely fetched him ! You know, for all their swank with their cottage-house dug-outs, the R.E.'s live on absolute garbage— that's why sappers never do any work."

" Yes, I know," grumbled Dooley ; " had half a dozen of 'em standing round while I was on the winter dug-outs this morning. Wouldn't do a stroke. Put up the ' expert-paid-to-give-advice-*only* ' tale. But they *did* look half-starved, too, now you mention it ! "

The meal progressed through the customary stages of tinned fruit, biscuits, and coffee. Then, having lit a cigarette, McKie rose and brushed the crumbs from his knees.

" Beastly cold wind ! " He shuddered. " And rain coming along, too. Just my luck, being ' on ' from one to three. Ough ! "

" Cheer up, Mac ! You've got a decent dug-out

to go to, anyway—more than *I* have," said Dooley; " and you never know your luck—the Turks *might* wake up and give you a show while you're ' on ' ! "

" Don't believe there *are* any Turks," growled McKie; " anyway, I've not seen one for long enough now."

" What ?   Why, Old Man Souliman Bey waved his fez to me out of their communication-trench only this morning ! *He's* there, anyway. *And* the boy who works the machine gun.   There might even be another, for all you know.   Don't look on the dark side, old thing !   Good-night."

" Good-night.   Come on, Anderson, and bring the lantern.   Oh, you can clear away now, Parker. Good-night."

" Good-night, sir," said Parker—his eye on the slices of pineapple still left in the tin.

.   .   .   .   .

To say that McKie was overjoyed when one o'clock came and brought with it a cold hand to pull away the blanket from his face, would be to over-tax the belief which we must assume the reader has in the enthusiasm of the British subaltern of the line.   He was distinctly annoyed, and his annoy-ance was not lessened by the sound of spattering rain driven before a roaring gale.

What he actually said, as he fumbled for the candle, is quite beside the point in any case, dealing as it did with the Turk alone, his habits, breeding, and ultimate destination.

Two hours of enforced wakefulness, mainly to be spent in the open air, lay before him. His duties were, after all, slight—merely to see that half a dozen sentries were as wakeful and as miserable as himself. A thankless task, he thought, as he pulled on his oilskin coat, and bending under the low doorway of the dug-out felt the beat of the cold rain in his face.

Framed between the close parapets of the trench the black silhouette of the hill loomed before him, backed by scudding clouds. At his side, almost part of the deep shadows which lurked between the walls of raw earth, a sleeping man muttered under his sodden blanket. McKie stooped and replaced the oilsheet which had slipped from the huddled form. Then he made his way up the narrow lane of shadows.

At intervals sentries were posted, their heads showing black against the sky as they gazed out towards the enemy; but for the most part the raised step on which they stood served as a sleeping-place for their fellows not yet on duty.

A shadow detached itself from the blackness before him. " All correct, sir," said a voice.

" That's good.   Much sniping going on ? "

" Just a bit, sir," said the sergeant, " but they turned our machine gun on to 'em about half an hour ago.   That cooled 'em off, like."

" Well, come on down the line with me, Sergeant."

They follow the windings of the trench, amongst the shadowy sleeping forms, down towards the cold gleam of the creaming wave-tops tossing murmuring out beyond the cliffs.   Biting gusts sweep down upon the pair as they pick their way, meeting the gale with bent heads.   Here and there a faint glimmer shows where the rain is splashing upon some stone on the edge of the parapet before finding its way to mingle with the shallow mud underfoot.

The journey is not a long one, and after a question or two to test the wakefulness and intelligence of a sentry, the sergeant returns to his post and McKie to the dug-out, where he had left a candle burning.   How cosy it looks, framed in the black side of the trench, the soft yellow glow showing up the hissing raindrops.

He stoops and enters, sinking with a sigh of relief on to the box which answers for a chair.

Twenty minutes to spend before his next round of inspection. What a chance for that luxury known in full only to the exile in evil conditions —a long, luscious " waking dream " of home. Home !

McKie sighed, and slowly lit a pipe.

.   .   .   .   .

The trout, cunning fellows, had found cool ledges of shady rocks under which to escape from the blaze of the August sun, so it was not the least good risking one's neck in craning over the parapet of the old stone bridge to look for them. The graceful green streamers of water-weed seemed to wave farewell as the small boy, after a last careful scrutiny, slid from his precarious perch on the stonework and paddled through the white dust towards the home lane.

All the drowsy sounds and scents of the summer hung lazily in the air. The hum of the solemn water-wheel turning its stately old beams, all shining wet in the sunlight, over and over, to shake off their shower of silver drops and sink from sight again, the buzz of the insects busy among the flowers of the hedgerow whose scents—ragged robin and nettles mingling with the white dust— filled all the warm air . . . *this* was the purity, the

T

freshness, the rich, clear calm that goes to make up an English summer day.

Along the lane, dappled and barred by the shadows of the tall elms, the boy wanders, with the air of the cheerful soul who can boast a day and a life but just begun.

Now he must investigate a bush from beneath which a kingfisher has darted, flashing like a blue spark over the rolling water of the river; now his small soul is stirred to the chase (heritage of every Briton) as a sly brown weasel vanishes into the tall grass at the roadside.

If only Rover were here!—but Rover is big, even for a collie, and it would be a jolly unfair business from the weasel's point of view. Hullo! that's a Red Admiral—or perhaps only a Tortoiseshell; anyway, it's bad form to chase it unless one has a green net and is a real naturalist.

Rounding the corner a full steady roar meets the wanderer and he stands for a while to watch the rushing water foaming over the weir in a thousand frothing jets and swirling away in creamy streamers where the river once more runs deep.

A wet muzzle thrust against his hand causes him to swing round, and there is Rover himself, wagging

Photo   *Cotswold Publishing Co.*
BUBNELL LANE, BASLOW.
The bridge mentioned in "A Night in a Ditch" (page 273).

Photo   *Cotswold Publishing Co*
BUBNELL COTTAGE, BASLOW.
The low wall in front of the cottage where he sat down.

[To face page 274

joyfully from the shoulders, and pleading almost vocally for attention.

"Get ready, Rover! One — two — three — *off!*"

The small, chubby legs twinkle down the lane, the collie's long, easy bounds carrying him abreast in the cloud of fragrant dust.

Not till they reach the green wicket of the low white cottage whose thatch is swept by the branches of a cool elm tree is the race considered won and lost. There, in the pleasant shade, the boy pulls up abruptly and seats himself on the low garden wall, his back to the tall hollyhocks and the roses which deck the sweet-smelling beds of the little garden. Rover, contented with all mankind, as summed up in one small, sunburnt sample, collapses with a comfortable thud at his feet, lays his head between his paws, and sighs to himself. . . .

.   .   .   .   .

A slow, shuffling step, heard between the rushing of the gale (or was it the old weir by the mill?) makes McKie turn his head. The sergeant is ready for another round of inspection, and has splashed to the door of the dug-out, where the candlelight shows warm, as a moth is drawn to a lamp. And McKie joins him in that cold and wet outer world where the sinfulness of erring man has finally and completely turned upside down and inside out the plans that an omnipotent Author of Peace and Lover of Concord had laid for his especial benefit.

CHAPTER XXXIV

CHRISTMAS PRESENTS

CHAPTER XXXIV

THE BELTON BULLDOGS—*Continued*

CHRISTMAS PRESENTS

Gallipoli.
November 7th, 1915.

THIS letter may never be finished, as Johnny Turk has borrowed some H.E. shells from somewhere and three have just dropped picturesquely round our dug-out, eliminating one of the company cooks and wounding a box of biscuits in several places.

Later.—Another has just burst harmlessly in front of us, frightening a sparrow and three flies; if this important success leaks out in Ottoman circles it will make a stir.

Later.—The fifth has arrived, some distance away. They have evidently lost the range, and no further anxiety need be expended.

Before going on to tell all the latest news,

let us talk about Christmas presents, shall we ? What to send to our "lads in the trenches," and so forth. In a literary effort of a few days ago I "suggested some new thoughts," as the Quakers say, but these were more of a fleshly nature, stomachsome, in fact. Well, I haven't very many original notions about what the right and proper things to send out here are, and for definite information on this point one naturally turns to the advertisement pages of any periodical available. Thus we find that these authorities (who really *ought* to know) implore (or rather order) you to send us soap, tobacco, bug-powder, fountain-pens, chewing-gum, Bibles, watches, oil-skins, razors, and C.A.C.—which leaves the discriminating mother whose means are limited to something under £1,000,000 wondering which of all these things she shall put her hard-earned money into. Well, if as a non-expert outsider I may offer a word of advice, I should recommend the last-named—razors. Or rather, one razor. Having thus solved the main problem in what must appear to a cutlery manufacturing family a very simple way, we turn once more to the advertising expert who, with a sweep of the pen, wipes out all but safety-razors as useless at the Front. In this I fully agree with him, after a painful course of shaving at the hands of a grimy sample of the private soldiery armed with a " non-safety " which it is impossible to keep sharp, owing to the sand which it has usually to chop through before it gets to the patient's whiskers. By the way—*does* one talk about shaving thus openly in the best drawing-rooms ? I believe it's not considered delicate, but I've been off drawing-room parades for so long that I really forget ! Well, to cut a long story (and middling long whiskers) short, I would like a Gillette Safety Razor, sold by all the leading Cash Chemists & Co. But see that it is a genuine Gillette; all the advertisements will tell you what to say if unscrupulous mongers of inferior goods try to palm off the useless " just as good " variety. The price, as usual, is the drawback—one guinea—but that, with an utter disregard of the value of money, I leave entirely for you to settle, merely pointing out that £1 1s. 0d. is a small price to pay for having your health and home guarded by a (properly shaven) British soldier.

You remember my telling you how I lost my other safety-razor during the show on the 21st August at Chocolate Hill. Well, now then—it's " up to you."

Words cannot express how sick we all are of sitting looking at the Turks and doing nothing more energetic.   Probably they're just as bored as we are and have just as little to write home about as we have—even less, in fact, as they don't keep Christmas and so can't fill two pages with demands for safety-razors !

I suppose, to use a rather overworked phrase, " all eyes are upon " events in Servia just now, and we, even if we were doing anything, should naturally be forgotten.   As a matter of fact, I don't see any probability of our doing anything very exciting yet, unless the Germans can get through and reinforce the Turks.   Then we should have to fight to keep our position and not be driven off this Peninsula altogether.

Strictly *entre nous*, and not for the Censor's ears, there's just a chance of our having our place here taken by new troops (City battalions and such), and getting a trip over to Servia pretty soon. Then let the Huns look out, for the Bulldogs will be amongst them, and I'm jolly sure we'd fight better against the race who did all those gruesome things in Belgium than we do against the Turk, who fights " clean," and is really, when you get to know him, quite lovable.   For instance, one of them the other day, feeling that life in the Turkish trenches was getting a little boring, came by night and handed himself over to one of the Bulldogs, then on sentry duty.

As dawn was breaking a really screamingly funny sight was on view in our (D Company's) lines: three grinning Tommies marching with fixed bayonets as escort to an elderly Ottoman gentleman, evidently thoroughly delighted with himself, his fez under his arm and salaaming with both hands to everyone he met ! He gave our interpreter some useful information, too, when he found himself unshot and well fed. They keep doing this, simply walking up to our lines at night and handing themselves over, knowing that they'll be well treated and probably better fed than if they stayed with their own people. One of the Bulldogs landed an officer this way during last week.

As I write these words a wasp is buzzing around the dug-out and a butterfly was seen in the lines this morning. The bushes are sprouting again, too, especially a weird thing like a holly-bush, on which grow ordinary acorns ! Everything in this bally clime is dotty. Whoever heard of such things as young wasps in November ? And the flies ! My goodness, you should have seen the jam-pot at lunch ! I guess they'll go on all through the winter, as they don't seem to mind the cold. At night they simply get together under the shelter of anything that will keep the dew off them and swarm, like ordinary bees. The roof of our mess dug-out is always black with them at night, and they only wake up when the sun gets out. I heard an illuminating remark from our platoon naturalist, Private Twigg, the other night. He was sitting in his little dug-out, the roof of which is a ground sheet, and was examining the crust of flies which had collected there, by the light of a candle. And thusly did Private Twigg soliloquise : " 'Undreds and 'undreds of 'em—all fair shiverin' wi' cold. 'Uddled together fer waarmth they is. An' there ain't much waarmth in a fly—take a *'ell* of a lot o' little flies fer to boil a kettle ! "

I must tell you more about Private Twigg some day.

CHAPTER XXXV

AFTERNOON TEA

CHAPTER XXXV

The Belton Bulldogs—*Continued*

AFTERNOON TEA

Gallipoli Peninsula.

Of course, being the celebrated Yorkshire landing, Suvla is much better run than anywhere else ! And even here things aren't too good. This is not the Suvla it was in August ; what with mules and stores and the other modern conveniences they have planted here there might not be a war on at all. The trenches themselves are getting monotonous, too, and you have to walk about half a mile from here to get any real excitement. We do sometimes get shelled where my dug-out is, but on top of the hill they get it every day.

I went paying calls the other day, and the man I went to call on said :   " You'd better come inside, the shells are due about now." Well, he'd hardly spoken before a big shrapnel came along—*whizz !*

We both dived inside his dug-out and he lay on top of me (me being the visitor—there's etiquette in these things), and so escaped being hit. The next that came along blew about four sandbags on to us, and my pal remarked : " They'll really start in a minute ! " Well, I was simply quivering with emotion as it was. Anyway, we put the sandbags back, and the next shell dropped slap into a group of fellows about ten yards away, blowing all the money out of one man's pocket and part of *him* along with it—horrid splash. The other man, an officer of one of the regiments in our brigade, simply vanished in a cloud of dust and we only found unimportant parts of him when we came to have a look round. Regular jig-saw puzzle he was, so we finally gave it up. By this time I was quite abject in my terror, and when they told me that a Taube was coming over I simply set off and ran like a rabbit down that hill. It turned out to be one of our own machines, and they caught me and brought me back to have a cup of tea with them. Owing to the shelling, they said, their tea-parties were losing popularity and they weren't going to miss a visitor when he did come. But I didn't make what you would call a really *good* tea.

Candles have run out and I'm using a lamp (?) made from rifle oil and a bit of an old shirt, to write by.   To avoid further eye-strain I'll now stop work for the night (my first night off in five).

CHAPTER XXXVI

PRIVATE TWIGG—NATURALIST

CHAPTER XXXVI

THE BELTON BULLDOGS—*Continued*

PRIVATE TWIGG—NATURALIST

November 10*th*, 1915.

HAS it ever occurred to you to consider the basis of that smooth and efficient working which has made the British Army the wonder and envy of the civilised world and placed us where we are to-day ? No, it never occurred to you—it wouldn't, of course. Then I shall write a long article on it, and serve you right !

The basis of our military supremacy is cohesion. (That sentence is good enough for the *Spectator*—or *Daily News*, anyway.)   Let me explain in parable.

When an exalted personage cuts himself shaving on a cold November morning—Monday, for choice —and reaches his desk at the War Office just in time (11.35 a.m.) to get a 'phone message about shells that " are not " and *ought* to be, and upsets the ink over his new piece of blotting-paper, then

293

he calls in the office-boy (generally a viscount at the very least) and gives him a bad ten minutes. Now then—this is where the cohesion begins.   The viscount office-boy gets his own back on some fellow-junior of lower social rank, and he in turn works his ire off on some subordinate department, who take it out of any official available by means of a rather nasty Army Form on any topic which may be handy.   Thus the ball is set rolling until finally mere brigadiers are involved in the general snarl. From them comes the echo to the C.O., to the company commander, and finally, *via* the subaltern and the company sergeant-major, to the N.C.O., who passes it through all ranks—sergeants, corporals, and lance-corporals after their kind—to the long-suffering private soldiery, who receive their dose with evil language and lay all the blame on the platoon butt.

And Private Twigg is our platoon butt.

A professional butt must be gifted with the capacity for letting blame trickle off after the manner of the proverbial duck, but the complete butt has always an additional safeguard to fall back upon and to occupy his mind when mere patience is exhausted.   Private Twigg's " second string " is natural history, and to this he flies when sore oppressed by the snarls of his fellow-men, echoed down from the War Office as already described.

I have told you about the flies and his theory regarding their temperature. He doesn't stop merely at entomology, either. For instance :

One night when we were engaged in our usual nocturnal pastime of digging trenches and dodging snipers' bullets, we were greeted by a strange, eerie wowling from among the thick bushes on the hillside. Between the frenzied strokes of our picks and thrusts of our shovels we paused to discuss what bird, beast of prey, or fish of the sea could be responsible for this weird caterwauling.

" Some pore feller 'it in the neck," was one suggestion.

" Wild cats out for blood," was another.

" Turks on the war-path " (apparently a reminiscence of Red Indian stories) was yet another.

Private Twigg merely grunted scornfully, so, feeling that he held the key to the mystery, I asked him his opinion.

" Jacko," he said with conviction.

" Yes, it *might* be a bird, of course," I agreed, not quite getting the drift of his suggestion.

" No, sir ; not a bird, sir."

[Here the Manuscript ends.]

LIEUT. E. Y. PRIESTMAN

SHEFFIELD SCOUTMASTER'S GALLANT STAND

Extract from the Sheffield Daily Telegraph, February 5th, 1916.

A THRILLING account has come to hand of a gallant stand made recently at Suvla Bay by a party of the 6th (Service) Battalion York and Lancaster Regiment, under the command of Second-Lieutenant E. Y. Priestman. This will be of interest locally, as a very large percentage of the recruits raised for this Battalion were residents of Sheffield and district. Lieutenant Priestman was a Sheffield Scoutmaster.

The account says : " Our trenches ran along the coast, near Jeffson's Post, and orders had been received for us to work along the furthermost sap to enable us to gain a portion of higher ground on the left of our sap. In order to do this it was necessary to leave our trenches at night, run forward with sandbags to the place marked, and dig in as rapidly as possible. On this particular night, Lieutenant Priestman and about thirty N.C.O.'s and men were detailed to make good this position. Leaving the trenches about 1.0 a.m., they gained the position without incident, and commenced to entrench as quietly as possible.

" Shortly afterwards the Turks rushed the position. Lieutenant Priestman did not retire, but opened a rapid fire, which kept the enemy at bay for a while, but, coming on again with a combined rush, they decimated the whole of the gallant little band. Lieutenant Priestman fell, fighting till the last, and Regimental Sergeant Warr was also killed whilst taking up a message to him.

" We attacked the position again in larger force next night, and succeeded in holding it. The bodies of Lieutenant Priestman and several men were discovered, all the wounded having been removed by the enemy.

" The captured position was named ' Priestman's Post ' by Headquarters, to commemorate the gallantry of this young officer, who was respected by all who knew him."

STUDIES FROM THE DARDANELLES

STUDIES FROM THE DARDANELLES

THE BRITISH NAVY IN ACTION:

AND THE BRITISH ARMY DITTO DITTO:

E.Y. RIESMAN:

5·0 A.M. "STAND TO"

16TH (WESTBOURNE) SHEFFIELD TROOP BOY SCOUTS STARTING ON A TREK.

FROM LETTER TO A BOY SCOUT

Sitting sadly in my dug-out the other day, I waxed poetic (an incurable disease which attacks me at rare intervals—*e.g.*, "The Aeroplane Duet") and after a few spasms wrote the enclosed, which of course is awful rot. It's *such* awful rot that I must ask you to keep it yourself and not pass it round—as I don't want everyone to see what a sentimental beast Mr. Priestman is. Or, better still, you might burn it! My only excuse is that I haven't had a Scout (or a boy of any kind) to talk to for nearly five months now—and we *were* going to have a grand old trek in the Lakes last autumn, weren't we?

MAP MAGIC

TO JIMMY

SOMEWHERE IN ENGLAND

(*N.B.*—" *Jimmy* " *is a purely imaginary person, and the verses are all rot, of course.*)

I

Time was when you and I, Jimmy,
Would confidently plan
Precise to the remotest speck
The scheme of some tremendous trek.
Say, *those* were times, old man!

X

II

Those were the times that taught us
        The Magic of the Map ;
Plain paper showed us parks of trees,
And contours banks of bilberries
        Planted by us, old chap.

III

Here, where a lifeless line of blue
        Wriggled and writhed and ran,
To tinkling tune the printer's ink
Became a brook, upon whose brink
        Rested our caravan.

IV

Over that Magic Map, Jimmy,
        We tasted all the joys
That waited but the glorious day
When warbling we should march away
        With all the other boys.

V

And then—with clash of arms, Jimmy,
        There dawned another Day,
When, answering the bugle-call,
Though sick at heart to leave you all,
        Alone I marched away.

VI

Yet sometimes through the starlight
        A magic whisper blew
Across the gulf that lies between
Me and the Land of Might-Have-Been,
        And brought me back to you.

VII

And sometimes I have dreamt, Jimmy,
    That in the starlit land
Those schemes no Fates can e'er undo
We'll work together, me and you,
    Just as we often planned.

VIII

Though years may steal your boyhood,
    Or shot should steal my breath,
What can destroy our Magic Map
Whose wondrous roads will lead, old chap,
    Beyond the realms of death ?

E. Y. P

KEEP   UNSPOTTED

Wriggling through the cover
  Where bracken and briar grow green,
Enemies' eyes are watching,
  Enemies' ears are keen.
Be wary and cautious and cunning,
  For a blunder will give you away ;
And the Scout who can keep " unspotted "
  Is the fellow who wins the day.

Wriggling up to manhood
  The struggle is just the same.
Scouts, remember the motto
  That you learnt in your stalking game—
Enemies still await you,
  But stick to the surest way ;
For the Scout who can keep " unspotted "
  Is the fellow who wins the day.

—(*Found amongst his papers when sorting over his effects.*)

PRINTED IN GREAT BRITAIN BY
THE ANCHOR PRESS LTD.
TIPTREE ESSEX.